RODALE'S COLOR HANDBOOK OF GARDEN INSECTS

squash pg. 90
diatomaceous earth

RODALE'S COLOR HANDBOOK OF GARDEN INSECTS

By Anna Carr

Rodale Press, Emmaus, Pa.

Library of Congress Cataloging in Publication Data
Carr, Anna, 1955–
    Rodale's color handbook of garden insects.
    Bibliography: p.
    Includes index.
    1. Insects, Injurious and beneficial—Identification. 2. Garden pests—Identification. 3. Organic gardening. I. Title.
SB931.C34   635'.04'97   79–4048
ISBN 0-87857-250-3

2 4 6 8 10 9 7 5 3 1

Cover photograph by Ann Moreton

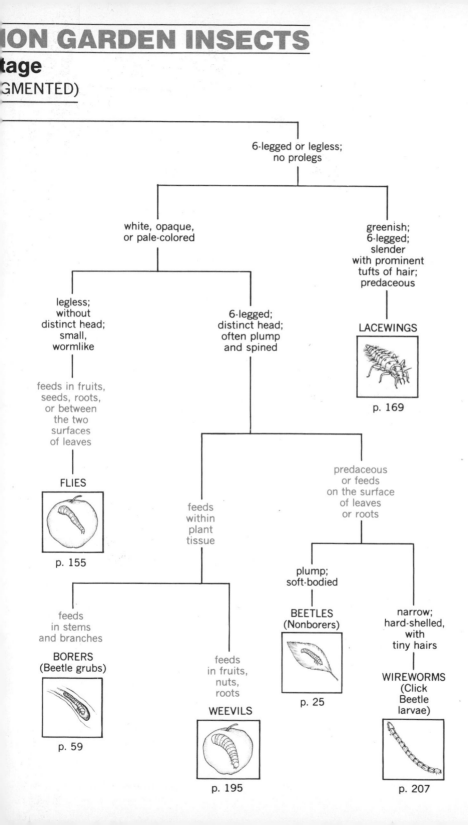

6-legged or legless;
no prolegs

white, opaque,
or pale-colored

greenish;
6-legged;
slender
with prominent
tufts of hair;
predaceous

LACEWINGS

p. 169

legless;
without
distinct head;
small,
wormlike

6-legged;
distinct head;
often plump
and spined

feeds in fruits,
seeds, roots,
or between
the two
surfaces
of leaves

FLIES

p. 155

feeds
within
plant
tissue

predaceous
or feeds
on the surface
of leaves
or roots

plump;
soft-bodied

BEETLES
(Nonborers)

narrow;
hard-shelled,
with
tiny hairs

p. 25

feeds
in stems
and branches

BORERS
(Beetle grubs)

feeds
in fruits,
nuts,
roots

WEEVILS

WIREWORMS
(Click
Beetle
larvae)

p. 59

p. 195

p. 207

CONTENTS

Acknowledgments vii

Introduction ix

How to Use This Book....................... xi

What Is an Insect?.......................... 1

How Insects Live and Grow.................. 2

Controlling Garden Insects 6

Aphids 9

Bees, Wasps, Ants, and Sawflies 15

Beetles 25

Borers..................................... 59

Bugs....................................... 75

Caterpillars................................. 93

Cicadas.................................... 141

Crickets, Grasshoppers, Mantids, and Walkingsticks.. 143

Earwigs.................................... 153

Flies 155

Lacewings.................................. 169

Leafhoppers, Treehoppers, and Spittlebugs........ 173

Mealybugs 181

Psyllids.................................... 185

Scales 187

Thrips..................................... 193

Weevils.................................... 195

Whiteflies 205

Wireworms 207

Non-Insects 209

Appendix: Common Fruits and Vegetables and the
Insects That Feed on Them.................... 216

For Further Reading......................... 227

Photograph Credits 228

Index...................................... 229

ACKNOWLEDGMENTS

This handbook represents the work of scores of insect enthusiasts across the country. Max E. Badgley, Lee Jenkins, Ray R. Kriner, Ann Moreton, Edward S. Ross, and many other photographers listed on the Photograph Credits page of this book sent over 5,000 color slides to me. They waited patiently while the pictures were reviewed and kept up a lively correspondence. Dr. William Olkowski corrected and advised me and acted as the sound "Voice of Science" during the writing of the book. In the early stages, Dr. Dan Dindall also supplied entomological advice and identified hundreds of insect slides. Dr. Ray Kriner helped put the finishing touches on the book as a whole. I would like to express my thanks to all of these people, to Thomas Quirk for his illustrations, to Mike Noll for the design, to Peggy Schneck who carried the book through production, and finally to Peggy MacNeil in whose garden I first watched a black swallowtail crawl from its chrysalis.

INTRODUCTION

If you were to spend an afternoon sifting through the soil and examining the plants in one square yard of your garden, chances are you'd find well over 2,000 insects, ranging from microscopic spring-tails to larger beetles and butterflies. Very few of these would pose any threat to the health and productivity of your garden. The fact is, most insects are directly beneficial to man and all are useful and necessary to the economy of nature. Insects aid in the decomposition of organic matter and in the formation of soil. They are responsible for the pollination of almost every fruit, flower, and vegetable crop. They keep weeds in check and provide us with silk, shellac, beeswax, honey, and other valuable products. If nothing else, they serve as food for birds, reptiles, small mammals, and other insects.

Then what about the insects we call "pests"? From a strictly ecological perspective, there are no such things. Webworms and bean beetles are as necessary to the natural balance of things as bees and earthworms. All living things have a special niche in the food chain. They are prey as well as predators.

As gardeners and farmers, we tend to forget this natural relationship among living things. We select the plants we want to grow, we determine how long they are going to live and what they will produce, and we nurture them to the exclusion of all other plants and animals. Native wildflowers that spring up in the garden become weedy competition to our crops and insects that feed on the plants or injure them in any way are our enemies. Sprayers and dusters in hand, we set about planning their demise.

It would be ridiculous to suggest that gardeners and farmers let weeds flourish or ignore the insects destroying their crops. When Nature takes over, she rarely has man's immediate needs in mind. But, more often than not, we indiscriminately kill all the insects we find in the garden, whether or not they are actually damaging the plants.In our obsession with destroying all possible competitors, we forget that most of the insects present are actually *helping* us produce food and that some plant-eating species are necessary to complete the food chain. Whether toxic chemical pesticides or natural poisons such as rotenone and pyrethrum are used, the results are much the same: Pesky species are eliminated and the insects, birds, and mammals that feed on them are also killed or leave the garden for greener pastures. The natural balance of predators, plant-eaters, and pollinators is disrupted.

It is hoped that this book will make you aware of the value of *all* garden insects and will inform you of their life cycles, their feeding habits, and the roles they play in the garden's ecology. Carry *Rodale's Color Handbook* into the garden. Learn the name of that insect on your squash plant and, before you take steps to shorten its life, decide whether or not it is really a pest. You might be doing yourself a favor by leaving the creature alone.

HOW TO USE THIS BOOK

The insects in this handbook are arranged in 19 groups on the basis of certain habits and superficial structural features obvious to gardeners. These are not directly related to the scientific groups but, to help you understand scientific relationships of these insects, the names of related scientific orders are mentioned in each chapter. Family names are listed where applicable and, beneath each entry, genus and species are given.

If you have the adult or larval form of an insect you wish to identify, refer to the flowcharts on the inside covers of the book. These charts will lead you to the proper chapter in which the insect is described and pictured. If the insect you want to identify is a six-legged adult, consult the chart in the beginning of the book. If it is a wormlike larva, turn to the chart in the back of the book. To follow the chart, simply begin at the top and select the description which fits your insect. Follow that line down to the next level and select the true statement there, and so on.

Next, turn to the appropriate chapter where the general habits and characteristics of the insect are described. Within the group, entries on specific insects are organized alphabetically. If the insect is a beetle, turn to the "Beetles" chapter and flip through until you spot the color photo of your insect.

If you see insect damage on plants but you aren't sure what caused it, turn to the Appendix in the back of the book. Here you will find lists of the common insects that feed on the foliage, fruit and flowers, or roots of that particular plant. This will help you know what sorts of insects are causing the damage.

Structure of a Typical Insect

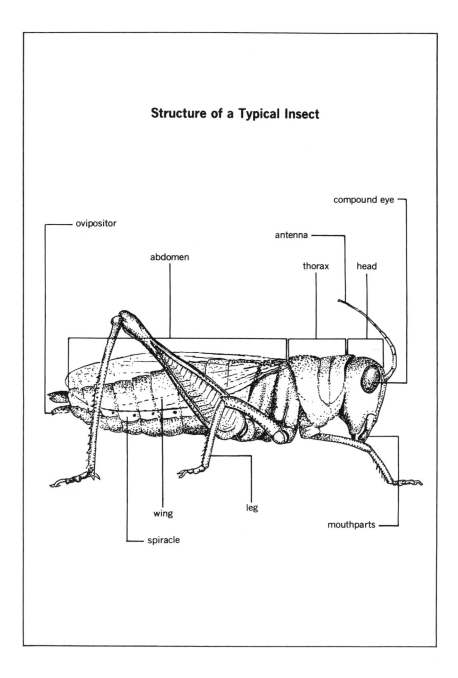

WHAT IS AN INSECT?

With over 4 million of them on each acre of the earth, it is surprising that few of us actually know what insects really are. For some reason, we want to place every little creature in this tremendous class — particularly if it is a pesky, creepy-crawly one. Spiders, centipedes, mites, millipedes, scorpions, ticks, and harvestmen are continually mistaken for insects when they are actually no more closely related to insects than lobsters or mollusks are. What then *is* an insect?

Basically, insects are small backboneless animals (invertebrates). They share certain physical characteristics that, together, distinguish them from all other animals.

Three body segments. Insects are usually elongate in form with three distinct sections of the body: *head, thorax,* and *abdomen.* The main sensing organs — eyes, antennae, and mouthparts — are on the head. The thorax bears wings and legs, and the abdomen has most of the digestive and reproductive organs as well as breathing holes called spiracles.

Outer skeleton. The body parts are sometimes difficult to detect since the insect's entire body is covered with a coat of armor. Instead of a backbone and skeleton as we know it, insects possess a hard, jointed frame on the outside of their body. This *exoskeleton* is made of chemical substances and proteins secreted by the insect's body. It is braced and ridged at various points to provide support as well as protection. Insoluble in water, alcohol, and most acids and enzymes, it provides a barrier to the world. It also makes the insect's body a rather clumsy package at times. Movement is difficult and growth can occur only when the exoskeleton is popped open during molts.

Six jointed legs. All insects have three pairs of legs attached to the thorax. This number gives the animal greater balance and mobility than any other. In walking, the insect moves the middle leg on one side of the body, together with the front and hind legs on the opposite side. This leaves three legs forming a stable tripod on the ground.

In addition to six legs, caterpillars have up to five pairs of plump, fleshy false legs that enable them to move more easily. These *prolegs* are hooked so that the larva can hang effortlessly from the host plant. Sawflies also have prolegs.

Two or four wings. Although many insects are wingless at some point in their lives, most adults possess one or two pairs of wings. The wings are actually part of the body wall. They begin as soft saclike outgrowths and later flatten and dry into solid membranous structures. They are supported by a framework of tubes and connected to the thorax by a series of muscles.

These four basic characteristics help to formally classify insects within the Animal Kingdom. Scientists group animals into major divisions on the basis of structure. The largest divisions are *phyla* which are subdivided into *classes.* Insects make up the class Insecta or Hexapoda (meaning six legged) of the phylum Arthropoda (meaning joint legged). Any animal with six jointed legs is an insect. Mites and spiders have jointed legs but they have eight, not six, of them. Hence, they belong to a different class in the phylum Arthropoda.

The Insect class is further divided into 26 *orders.* Orders are large groups of insects that share similar wing structures. Members of the order Coleoptera (beetles), for instance, are distinguished by a front pair of leathery or brittle wings that meet in a straight line down the center of the back. Insects belonging to the order Hemiptera (true bugs) possess front wings that are partly thickened and partly membranous. The order name appears beneath each chapter head.

1

Each order contains one or more *families*. The family name always ends in *idae* and refers to some particular feature its members share. Beetles belonging to the family Buprestidae are hard-bodied, brightly colored, metallic insects. In the larval stage, they have a flatheaded appearance and are known as the flatheaded wood borers. Members may look exactly alike or they may resemble one another only slightly, but all have a flat head.

The most fundamental levels of classification and the ones that are most used to identify insects are the *genus* and *species*. The genus name refers to a small group of closely related members of a family. It is always capitalized. The species name is seldom capitalized. It refers to a single insect that can be distinguished from others in the genus by a particular feature or habit. Thus, both the asparagus beetle and the spotted asparagus beetle belong to the genus *Crioceris* but, since their markings and their habits are slightly different, they are distinguished by separate species names: *asparagi* and *duodecimpunctata*. These, together with the genus name, are the insects' formal names. In this handbook, they appear just below the common name at the top of each insect entry.

HOW INSECTS LIVE AND GROW

Since their bodies are encased in rigid shells, insects cannot grow gradually as we do. Instead, they grow in stages. They feed until their coat becomes too tight, then they stop eating and rest while it splits open. Meanwhile, a new shell has formed beneath the original one so, when the insect crawls out of its old armor, it is already protected. This is called *molting*. After molting, it feeds voraciously until it outgrows this new shell, then molts again. In this way, it gradually increases in size. The form of the insect between each molt is called an *instar*. Most insects pass through three to six instars. However, depending upon temperature and food supply, there may be up to 30 instars before the insect reaches maturity.

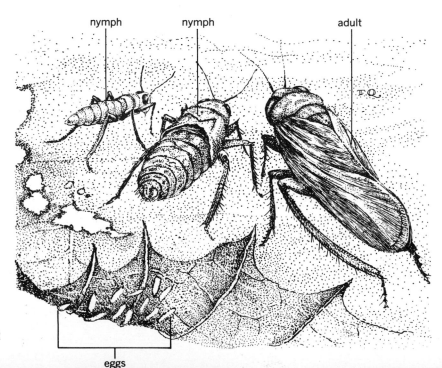

nymph   nymph   adult

eggs

Insects are not born with all their adult features. They acquire these during certain moltings and pass through a series of "form changes." This process is known as *metamorphosis.* True bugs; grasshoppers, crickets, and mantids; earwigs; thrips; whiteflies; aphids; and scales pass through three basic forms — *egg, nymph,* and *adult.* This is called simple or *incomplete metamorphosis* (fig. 2). This is because the nymph more or less resembles the adult form, but it does not possess fully developed wings and its coloring may be quite different. After a series of molts in which it increases in size, it molts a final time, acquiring wings and fully developed antennae. It emerges as a full-fledged adult.

Most other insects, including bees and wasps; beetles; butterflies and moths; flies; and lacewings have *complete metamorphosis* (fig. 3) in which they pass through four distinctly different life stages — *egg, larva, pupa,* and *adult.* Immature forms known as larvae bear no resemblance to the adult form. They are more or less wormlike and may be legged or legless. Sometimes they are covered with spines or tufts of hair. They have chewing mouthparts, even if the adult counterpart has sucking mouthparts. They molt several times, increasing in size but very little in form.

After the molt of the last instar, the larva changes into an inactive form called the *pupa.* It stops feeding and may even stop moving. Some insects spin a cocoon or web or roll a leaf around their bodies to protect themselves during this period of vulnerability.

During pupation, the insect changes profoundly from larva to adult. Some structures and tissues such as the plump little false legs dissolve and new features such as legs, wings, and antennae develop. When the adult features have been formed, the insect splits its pupal chamber and emerges. Later, wings dry, pigmentation develops, and armor hardens.

The adult stage of insects with either type of metamorphosis is usually a relatively short one, geared entirely toward reproduction. Some adult forms such as male scale insects do not even have mouths since they live such a short time and do not need to eat. They mate and die almost immediately afterward.

Although adulthood is usually the shortest period of the insect's life, it is often the one in which the insect is most aware of the world around it. The nervous system is fully developed and vision is at its best. Respiration, circulation, and, if the insect has mouthparts, digestion, are in full swing. Often, insects are most mobile during adulthood.

Breathing. Insects do not have lungs. In almost all species, the blood contains no hemoglobin and is not used to carry oxygen. Instead, insects breathe through tiny holes or *spiracles* in the thorax and abdomen (fig. 1 on page xii). Oxygen passes through a system of branching tubes to all parts of the body. Sometimes the insect pumps its abdominal muscles in order to encourage ventilation.

Circulating the blood. Insect blood is a yellowish green or clear, thick fluid. It carries food to body organs, stores proteins and water, and picks up waste materials for excretion. It is pumped by a simple, tubular heart located in the middle of the back, just beneath the body wall. Since there are no arteries or veins, the blood sloshes through the insect's body cavity, percolating back and forth from the head to the abdomen, bathing every organ. It moves into the wings through rigid tubes.

Eating and digesting. Insects feed on all kinds of things — dead and living plants and animals, paper, trash, and fabrics. Some dine only on blood or eat just a particular layer of cells in a particular kind of leaf. Others consume anything and everything.

The mouthparts needed to break down these foods are complicated and specialized. There are two basic types — those that chew food and those that suck it. Insects that chew their food have sturdy jaws which move sideways.

3

Complete Metamorphosis

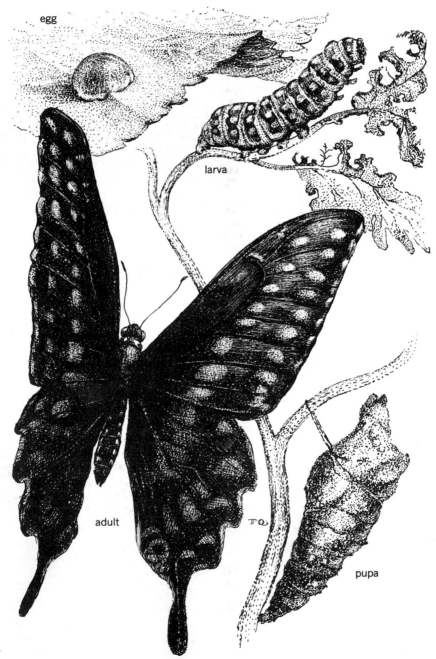

egg

larva

adult

pupa

4

The jaws are toothed and can be used to tear food as well as mash and chew it. An additional set of jaws holds the food when the main jaws are open and serves as a kind of scoop that gets the stuff into the insect's mouth.

Insects that suck their food have long, styluslike mouthparts. Most garden insects with sucking mouthparts pierce the surface of the plant or animal material with a hollow, jointed beak. One or more tiny needles within this beak make holes in the tissue. Some insects such as butterflies and moths, lack these piercing organs. They have a long, retractable tube or *proboscis* through which nectar is siphoned.

Ingested food passes from the mouth into a simple canal where, if necessary, it is broken down by enzymes. Carbohydrates such as nectar are soluble in water and can be incorporated in body fluids immediately. They provide instant sugar energy while fats must be digested and carried to storage muscles before they can provide energy. Since insects have fairly dry bodies, they can only dissolve a small amount of sugar and, gram for gram, they get little energy from it. Fat is a much better long-term energy source. Insects that fly at high speeds for long periods of time, are usually fat-eaters. Butterflies that fly slowly or flower flies that move in quick, short jaunts feed on nectar.

Tasting. Insects have taste organs on lips enclosing their jaws and on special feelerlike organs behind the jaws. Some insects use their antennae to taste things and certain butterflies have taste buds in their feet. These are so sensitive that, as the insect lands on a flower rich in nectar, the proboscis automatically uncoils.

Butterflies are not the only insects with an acute sense of taste. Most other insects are very sensitive to slight differences in salt or sugar content or in the particular flavor of their preferred food. Leaves treated with bitter-tasting or acidic substances are rejected by the insects that normally feed on them.

Smelling. The sense of smell is also very acute in most insects. Many secrete substances whose odors repel enemies or attract mates. Although we cannot detect these odors, other insects can and even in the most infinitesimal amounts, the smells excite them.

Hearing. Insects hear by means of a delicate drum or *tympanum* built into the body wall. This thin membrane connects to special internal organs that carry impulses to the tiny "brain" in the insect's head. Grasshoppers and crickets have very large tympana; others have drums so small they are almost invisible. Sound receptors are also present in the antennae of certain insects or in the tiny hooks on their abdomens.

Touching. Insects have thousands of sensory hairs scattered over the surface of their bodies. These are connected to nerve endings. They tell the insect about its surroundings and inform it about its body position. For instance, when an insect bends its leg, it bends the hairs located there. These send messages to the "brain," informing the insect that the leg is bent. Scales and hairs on the wings of a butterfly or moth tell the insect how to fold its wings when alighting. They also seem to be sensitive to air movements during flight.

Seeing. Insects have extremely large, complicated eyes that take up a large portion of the insect's head, yet are very inefficient. They are made up of many separate hexagonal lenses fitted closely together. Each lens is connected to a cone that directs the light to a series of eye cells. The lens "sees" just a portion of the image. Nerve impulses in the brain build the fragments into a compound picture that has something of a jigsaw puzzle effect.

These eyes can detect movement quite well, but they do not produce a particularly clear picture because there is no focusing mechanism. They are sensitive to color, enabling many pollinating insects to have "favorite" flower colors. Some bees will pollinate only red flowers. Others prefer yellow or blue. Beetles, whose eyesight is quite poor, make few distinctions in color and are as attracted to white or pale flowers as they are to brightly colored ones. Some insects are so sensitive to color that they can see ultraviolet light that appears black to us.

In addition to compound eyes, most insects possess simple, single-lensed eyes called *ocelli*. These tiny organs perceive light but produce no image. In adults and nymphs, they lie at the base of the antennae or on top of the head. In larvae, ocelli are located on each side of the head. Since they possess no compound eyes, larvae rely entirely on these primitive organs for their vision.

Flying. Insect wings are attached to the thorax by a set of sophisticated flight muscles. The wings themselves, unlike those of birds, contain no muscles. Instead, all movement is controlled by ball-and-socket joints and thoracic muscles that enable the wing to turn in almost any direction and, depending on the species, beat 10 to 1,000 times per second. Insects can loop the loop, swoop, fly upside down, back up in midair, hover, or stop suddenly. Some can move each pair of wings separately while others move them together. They can even twist the wing surfaces to provide lift and thrust during flight.

CONTROLLING GARDEN INSECTS

Once you are aware of the basic ways in which insects function you can begin to understand their behavior in the garden. You can learn to recognize when they are helping crop production and to predict when they might become pestiferous. Remember, insects are not pests simply because they eat crop plants: They become pests when their populations get out of hand and they actually injure plants and interfere with their capacity to produce food. With a little care and thought, you can learn to *prevent* most infestations of possible pests, to *tolerate* the presence of some plant-eating species, and to *control* them when they begin to cause intolerable damage.

Garden maintenance. Many of your insect "problems" can be eliminated by proper garden maintenance. Although weeds, trash, diseased plant material, and unplowed soil invite many beneficial insects into the garden, they also encourage pestiferous species. Insects seek shelter in weeds and lay eggs in and around them. They hibernate in garden trash and in the first few inches of untilled soil. Using a clean mulch and keeping the garden well weeded, but not necessarily "weed free," not only makes for healthier plants, but also controls the growing populations of certain insects. Plowing the soil nine or ten inches deep in early spring or fall exposes some of the larvae and pupae to the elements and they die.

Diversified planting. You can help prevent an overpopulation of particular plant-eating insects through diversified planting. Most insects feed on plants belonging to a certain family and reject unrelated ones. By interplanting favorite host plants with other types, you keep the increase of pest populations at a minimum. For instance, cucumber beetles don't enjoy much except cucumber, squash, and melon, so plant these crops amidst corn or pole beans. Cabbage loopers may nibble on many different plants, but they rarely stay long on anything other than broccoli, cabbage, kale, and other curcurbits. Avoid planting these crops together. Instead, interplant them with unrelated ones. Some plants such as aromatic herbs, onion, garlic, and certain flowers planted around garden crops are believed to repel insects.

Crop rotation. Since many insects hibernate or lay overwintering eggs in or on their host plants, it is a good idea not to plant the same crop in the same place each season. Although it is hard to avoid this in a small garden, try to rotate crops as much as possible.

Of course, none of these practices completely eliminate plant-eating insects from your garden. That is the last thing you should do. The idea is not to have an insect-free garden, but merely to limit the number of potentially destructive species so that they can be kept in control by natural predators. All insects are beneficial, even if they seem to be injurious to crop plants. Garden plants can tolerate incredible foliage loss and damage from insects.

Altered planting times. You can alter planting times so that crops grow when they are less likely to be injured by certain insects. Observe insect cycles closely and keep records of when eggs are laid, larvae emerge, and when feeding is heaviest. In this way, you can take advantage of insects' natural cycles by planting crops before or after the pests have passed through their hungriest period. Also consider when plants are most susceptible to injury — when they are weakest and most vulnerable — so that their hardiest time coincides with the insect's hungriest period.

Barriers. You can discourage insects present in the garden from laying eggs or feeding on certain plants by setting up barriers between them and your plants. Aluminum foil wrapped around a tree trunk prevents borers from crawling up the trunk. A band of the commonly available adhesives Stikem or Tanglefoot catches moths and flies as they lay eggs. Netting keeps fruit flies away from fruit bushes and discourages many insects from laying eggs on certain host plants. Paper collars wrapped around the stems of transplants prevent cutworm damage.

Resistant varieties. If you select *resistant varieties* of crop plants, chances are few insects will become serious garden pests. These specially bred, horticultural varieties are unattractive to certain potential pests or are at least able to withstand much more insect injury than other varieties of the species. Of course, no variety is completely resistant to all pests, but often some are capable of resisting and tolerating the insects more than others. Check seed catalogs for varieties resistant to the insects that might become problems, and run your own experiments to determine the best varieties for your garden.

Sprays. Insects inevitably get out of hand even after all the preventative measures have been taken. As our tolerance, and the plant's, begin to run low, most of us reach for the spray can. Before applying any kind of poison we should ask ourselves, is this *really* necessary? Before spraying, try some of these simple, harmless yet effective control measures.

In the home garden, most insects can be picked by hand and dropped into a jar of kerosene or simply squashed between the thumb and forefinger. Check plants frequently and eliminate the eggs of pestiferous insects. This is much better than spraying since it kills only the specific insect in question and allows the beneficial insects to live.

If you *must* spray, try clear water first. Sprayed forcefully on foliage, it helps control aphids, mites, and many other small leaf-eating insects that feed in out-of-the-way places. If this does not work, add a little Fels-Naphtha soap to the water. This will act as a kind of mild contact insecticide and repellent to not only aphids and mites, but some leafhoppers, leafminers, and caterpillars as well. Buttermilk dissolved in water may also reduce populations of some insects, as will any number of herbal or aromatic plant infusions. A tea made from garlic and water is said to repel some insects. Cedar chips brewed in warm water kills Mexican bean beetles and squash bugs. Flour added to the water controls many different caterpillars and grubs since it sticks to their soft, damp bodies and eventually smothers them as it dries.

In the orchard, premixed dormant-oil sprays help to smother many leaf-eating insects that feed in hard-to-reach places. This mixture is sprayed on trees before buds open in the spring or after leaves have fallen in the autumn. In this way, the delicate buds and young growth are not damaged.

As a last resort, more high-powered, naturally occurring insecticides and bacteria may be necessary. Although these are not as harmful as most of the chemical poisons, they are nevertheless toxic and should be used only when the situation has truly grown out of hand.

Bacillus thuringiensis is a bacteria that can be purchased in most garden stores and used to control various caterpillars. It is sold under the tradenames Dipel and Thuricide. Dusted on infested plants, it is eaten and enters the insect's stomach where it penetrates the lining and multiplies in the bloodstream. The caterpillars stop feeding, become paralyzed, and gradually weaken and grow sick until they finally dry up and die. *Bacillus popullae* is a similar bacteria sold under the tradename Doom. It is primarily used against Japanese beetle grubs and is applied to turf areas.

Diatomaceous earth, sold as Perma-Guard, is made from the ground skeletons of small fossilized animals. When soft-bodied insects such as ants, aphids, beetle grubs, boxelder bugs, caterpillars, fly maggots, mites, slugs, or thrips eat it, their stomachs are punctured. This causes the insects to die from dehydration. It is probably the safest, most effective contact insecticide, but is very expensive.

False hellebore is a botanical insecticide that is sold as a dry powder and can be applied as a spray (1 ounce of hellebore dissolved in 2 gallons of water) or a dust mixed with hydrated lime and flour. It works as a stomach poison in many chewing insects such as grasshoppers, beetles, caterpillars, and sawflies.

Pyrethrum is a contact botanical insecticide, not a stomach poison, and is effective against many different insects, including leafhoppers, aphids, caterpillars, bugs, and various beetles. It is a particularly useful orchard spray. Since it is an extremely potent pesticide, use it only when absolutely necessary.

Rotenone is another botanical insecticide that kills many kinds of insects but does not harm warm-blooded animals. Since it has little lasting effects, it must be reapplied periodically. A 1 percent solution should kill any insects.

Ryania, made from the roots of a tropical shrub, is a potent insecticide which can be used if all else fails. It is sometimes recommended for use against certain orchard pests and works against a variety of insects. It is very potent and should not be used unless other methods have failed.

Sabadilla dust is effective in controlling a number of insects with a minimum of danger, but it is not as easy to find as some of the other plant-derived pesticides. It kills aphids, caterpillars, some beetles, and bugs on contact.

None of these insecticides should be used unless all other control methods have failed. Read about them in garden pest books such as *Organic Plant Protection* (Emmaus, Pa.: Rodale Press, 1976) and seek the advice of extension agents. Even the most "natural" sprays can seriously upset the natural balance in your garden if they are improperly or carelessly applied.

APHIDS

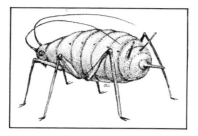

HOMOPTERA

Aphids are familiar to gardeners everywhere. Soft-bodied, pear-shaped insects less than $1/10$ inch long, they constitute a very large group of sucking insects. They may be winged or wingless. Usually, they possess a pair of tiny tubes at the end of the abdomen. Through these, aphids spray a waxy fluid in the face of their enemies. They also excrete honeydew or excess sap. Since ants are attracted to this substance, they are often present with aphids. In exchange for the honeydew, ants protect the aphids from predators and carry them to new plants when food runs low.

The life cycle of most species is rather complex. Eggs laid in fall hatch the following spring. Immediately, the nymphs begin piercing plant tissue and extracting sap. They pile on top of one another and feed in masses. The first generations consist entirely of females that give birth to live young without being fertilized by males. Eventually, the aphids begin to crowd out one another and a generation of winged females appears. These migrate to a new host plant where they feed and produce many more generations of wingless females. Toward the end of the summer, when the population density has increased again and temperatures have begun to drop, a generation of true males and true females appears. These individuals mate and the females lay eggs on the present host plant or on another. Eggs overwinter and hatch the following spring.

By this complex system, aphids build up tremendous populations over a relatively short period of time. Were it not for their many natural parasites and predators, they would have overrun the world long ago. Entomologists estimate that, if all the descendants of a single aphid lived and reproduced, there would be over 5 billion by the end of the summer. Fortunately, ladybird beetles, lacewings, and syrphid flies keep these insects under control. You can control the adults by dusting with diatomaceous earth. Aluminum foil placed on the ground under young plants prevents aphid damage and viral transmission to curcurbits and peppers.

APHID
Bean Aphid
Aphis fabae

Badgley / *A. fabae*

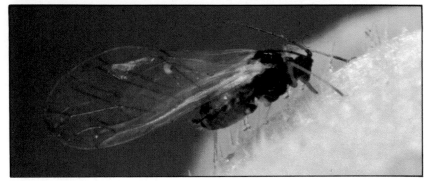

Badgley / *A. gossypii*

Range: This and similar species throughout North America.

Description: Dark green to bluish black; $\frac{1}{12}$ inch long.

Life Cycle: Many generations per year. Hibernation occurs in the egg stage.

Host Plants: Bean, beet, chard, pea, rhubarb, spinach.

Feeding Habits: Aphids congregate on succulent foliage and stems. Leaves turn yellow and the plant is generally weakened.

Natural Controls: Spray foliage with soapy water, then rinse with clear water.

$\overline{\frac{1}{12}}''$

APHID
Green Peach Aphid/Spinach Aphid
Myzus persicae

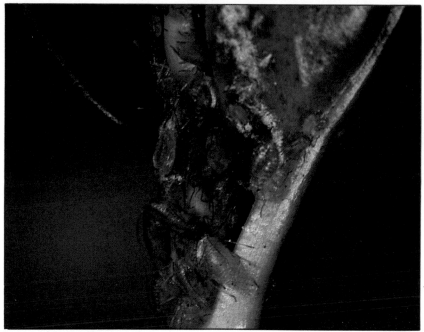

Badgley / Adults

Range: Throughout North America.

Description: Greenish to pink or red, or dark brown with wings; $\frac{1}{10}$ to $\frac{1}{5}$ inch long.

Life Cycle: Innumerable generations per year. In the North, hibernation takes place in the egg stage, elsewhere females reproduce continuously.

Host Plants: Many small fruits, garden vegetables, and orchard crops.

Feeding Habits: Aphids suck the juices of leaves and stems and transmit viral diseases.

Natural Controls: Spray foliage with water, soapy water, or use rotenone for serious infestations.

$\frac{1}{5}''$

APHID
Pea Aphid
Acyrthosiphon pisum

Badgley / Colony

Badgley / Winged adult

Badgley / Wingless adult

Range: Throughout North America.

Description: Green; ⅕ inch long.

Life Cycle: Ten to 20 generations per year. Winter is passed in the egg stage on field crops or weeds.

Host Plants: Bean, pea.

Feeding Habits: Aphids can become abundant on plants and can cause serious damage to foliage and pods.

Natural Controls: Spray foliage with soapy water, then rinse with clear water.

⅕″

APHID
Woolly Apple Aphid
Eriosoma lanigerum

Henley / Adult

Oregon / Damage

Jenkins / Eggs

Range: Throughout North America.

Description: Purplish, covered with a bluish white, cottony substance; $^1/_{10}$ inch long. EGGS: Laid on bark.

Similar Insects: Mealybugs (pp. 181–84).

Life Cycle: Many generations per year. Winter is passed in the egg stage.

Host Plants: Apple, pear, quince.

Feeding Habits: Aphids feed on trunk and branches, covering them with cottony material. Twigs become swollen. Infested roots develop nodules, causing saplings to become stunted.

Insect Predators: Chalcid wasp (*Aphelinus mali*).

Natural Controls: In early spring, spray trees with dormant-oil spray.

$\overline{^1/_{10}{''}}$

BEES, WASPS, ANTS, AND SAWFLIES

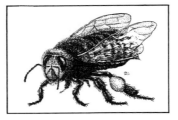

HYMENOPTERA

Almost every insect in this well-known, highly socialized order is an active predator, parasite, or pollinator. Only the sawflies qualify as serious garden or orchard pests and they are kept in check by a cousin, the tiny ichneumon wasp that drills through several inches of wood to parasitize them.

Bees, wasps, sawflies, and some ants are best recognized by their two pairs of transparent wings. In flight, these are fastened together by a row of tiny hooks, creating a single wing surface. This makes it easy to confuse the insects with flies which have only one pair of wings.

Mouthparts are basically the chewing type, often with an additional tonguelike structure through which nectar and honeydew are siphoned. Adults of some species, including most parasitic ones, rely on nectar, honeydew, and pollen for their food, although the larvae may be carnivorous. In the case of honey bees and bumble bees, the legs are fitted with a special basket structure and a rake for collecting pollen. Wasps and sawflies lack these features but they nevertheless aid in plant breeding since some pollen inevitably collects on their legs and abdomen as they feed. Ants are primarily scavengers that play no role in pollination.

Metamorphosis is complete. Although reproduction is primarily by mating, often males are produced from unfertilized eggs. This is known as *parthenogenesis.* In mating, the female collects the sperm in a special abdominal chamber. She stores them and releases them only when instinct tells her that more fertile eggs, and hence more females are needed.

Identification within the order is fairly straightforward. Ants are recognized by their enlarged abdomen. Bees and wasps can be separated from sawflies by the narrow waist that connects the thorax with the abdomen. Wasps can be distinguished from bees by their lack of hair. They are generally thinner than bees and more delicately formed.

All sorts of life histories and habits are represented by this order, from the highly structured, industrious lives of the ants, social bees, and wasps, to the independent lives of certain solitary species.

Ants have one of the most complex social lives of all animals. Each colony consists of three castes — males, workers, and females. Males mate with winged females, then die before their wives lose their wings and found new colonies. Each new queen produces a brood of workers which soon matures and begins feeding the queen and tending new larvae. They gather food and create new galleries for the nests.

The list of "high society" bees and wasps is led by the aristocratic *honey bees.* Their communities of up to 80,000 individuals are governed by a single queen who alone is capable of reproduction. Most members of the colony are sterile females or workers who maintain the hive, groom the queen, and gather nectar and pollen to feed the young. Since they visit only one kind of flower on 15 each trip, they are proficient pollinators and a great deal of fruit and vegetable production relies upon their efforts.

Typically, the first broods consist entirely of infertile females. Males or drones appear in the second or third generation and finally, toward the end of the season, fertile females are produced. Upon hatching, the sisters drive their mother from the hive and fight to be the colony's new queen. The survivor then flies off to mate and returns to settle her hive for the long winter.

Unlike honey bees which are maintained through the winter by an elaborate method of vibrating their wings to keep warm, *bumble bee* colonies disband in fall. Theirs are much smaller colonies than those of the honey bee, rarely exceeding populations of two or three hundred. They are equally efficient pollinators with large pollen "baskets" on their hind legs and plenty of ravenous young to feed. Their life cycle differs from that of honey bees in that the young queens do not fight and kill one another. Instead, most of the sisters leave the hive and find mates of their own. The old queen and all her workers perish in the fall, leaving only the young, mated queens to start new colonies the following spring.

Social wasps, such as *yellow jackets* and *hornets,* also die in the winter, leaving only the queen to hibernate in garden trash. Also like the bees, adults feed on nectar and pollen, but they use their well-developed jaws to capture insects that they feed to the legless young workers. The young chew the food and swallow most of it, but give some to the adults. In this way, they help digest the adults' food.

Workers make up most of the colony. They gather food and feed and care for the young. Toward the end of the season, white-faced males appear along with true, virgin females. The males are extremely docile, stingless creatures. With the beginning of fall, worker wasps stop feeding any larvae that are too young to mature before winter. They destroy the nest and die with the first hard freeze.

Solitary species that do not form colonies include bees such as *mason bees, leafcutting bees,* and *carpenter bees.* They nest in the soil, often so close to one another that they seem to form a colony. However, each goes his own way and there is no cooperation or division of labor. These insects are rare visitors to the garden.

Some solitary wasps are important garden inhabitants. A few, such as the *mud dauber wasp,* build nests where they nourish the young until maturity. After laying her eggs, the female solitary wasp hunts for spiders, crickets, cicadas, flies, or leafhoppers which she paralyzes, injecting a kind of preservative venom, and brings home. Just before sealing the egg cells, she drops an insect into the pot. This gives each larva a ready source of food.

Other wasps do not build nests, preferring to deposit their eggs on the bodies of host insects. Since they have very high reproductive rates and are capable of destroying many different insect pests, these insects are extremely valuable control agents. *Chalcid, braconid,* and *ichneumon wasps* are just a few of the important members of this group. Their thin, very small larvae begin to feed as soon as they hatch within the body of their prey. Gradually, they gain weight and begin to turn the color of their host's blood. They have no eyes or true legs and their heads consist almost entirely of jaws. Species that feed within a host usually hibernate there, but others pass the winter as mature larvae or pupae outside their host.

The more obvious, yet much less beneficial, group of solitary insects is the *sawflies.* Eggs of these insects are deposited in stems, buds, or leaves which the female cuts with a special saw on the tip of her abdomen. Eggs hatch into larvae that resemble caterpillars but have more than five pairs of false legs. They feed for several weeks before maturing. After a brief mating period, they die. To protect tree crops from these insects, apply a rotenone spray when flower petals begin to fall.

Ross / Adults "herding" aphids

Range: Various species throughout North America.

Description: Black, brown, or reddish; wingless or winged with an enlarged abdomen; ⅙ to ¼ inch long.

Life Cycle: Eggs are laid continuously throughout the spring, summer, and fall. Colonies hibernate in the soil or in garden trash.

Feeding Habits: Most garden ants feed on organic matter, although a few species prey on other insects. Many feed on the honeydew secreted by aphids. They may become a nuisance since they "herd" aphids, protecting them from enemies and transporting them to new host plants. Control of aphids will generally eliminate the ant problem.

¼"

BEE
Bumble Bee
Bombus sp.

Ross / Adult

Range: Various species throughout North America.

Description: Black, sometimes with yellow bands on the abdomen; fuzzy; spurs on the hind legs; ⅓ to 1 inch long. EGGS: Laid on or in the ground.

Life Cycle: Several broods per year. Most die in winter; only the young queens remain to hibernate in protected spots.

Feeding Habits: Workers feed on nectar of many plants and are valuable pollinators. Since they visit many different plant species on each gathering trip, they are less efficient than honey bees.

1″

BEE
Honey Bee
Apis mellifera

Seip / Adult

Range: Throughout North America.

Description: Brownish yellow with darker thorax covered with short hair, some species are black; ¼ to ½ inch long.

Life Cycle: Eggs are laid continuously except during extremely cold periods. All forms hibernate in the hive.

Feeding Habits: Worker bees feed on nectar from many different plants and, in the process, transfer pollen from one flower to another or from the male flower part to the female. Their pollinating is particularly important in orchards.

½″

19

SAWFLY
European Apple Sawfly
Hoplocampa testudinea

Kriner / Damage

Badgley / Larvae

Range: Eastern United States with similar species throughout North America.

Description: Brownish yellow with a black spot on the head; ⅕ inch long. EGGS: White; shiny; laid on blossoms. LARVA: White to tan with a dark brown head.

Similar Insects: Pear sawfly (p. 21).

Life Cycle: One brood per year. Hibernates in cocoons in the soil.

Host Plants: Apple.

Feeding Habits: Larvae mine fruit, leaving brown sawdust on the surface.

Natural Controls: For serious problems, spray rotenone as soon as flower petals begin to fall and repeat two weeks later.

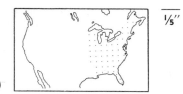

⅕"

SAWFLY
Pear Sawfly
Hoplocampa brevis

Oregon / Adult

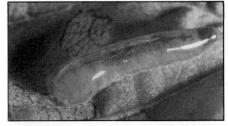

Oregon / Larva

Oregon / Damage

Range: Eastern United States.

Description: Brown with yellowish wings; ⅕ inch long.

Similar Insects: European apple sawfly (p. 20).

Life Cycle: One brood per year. Pupae overwinter in cocoons in the soil.

Host Plants: Pear, quince.

Feeding Habits: Larvae bore into developing fruits, but seldom cause serious damage.

⅕"

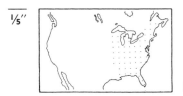

WASP
Braconid Wasps
Braconidae

Ross / Adult

Ross / Cocoons

Range: Various species throughout North America.

Description: Black, yellowish, or red; $\frac{1}{10}$ to $\frac{1}{4}$ inch long. EGGS: Laid in the bodies of hosts. LARVA: White; wormlike, develop within the host.

Life Cycle: Usually several generations per year. Most species hibernate as larvae or pupae in their hosts.

Feeding Habits: Adults lay eggs on the larvae of various caterpillars or aphids. Larvae may feed within the hosts or on the surface. Often brown cocoons are seen on the backs of hornworms and other caterpillars.

$\frac{1}{4}''$

Ross / Adult

Range: Various species throughout North America.

Description: Black and yellow with clear wings folded along the length of the body when at rest; ½ to ¾ inch long. EGGS: Laid in papery cell colonies made of plant materials glued together and formed in hollow logs or stumps.

Life Cycle: Colonies disperse in fall and young mated queens hibernate in bark, forming new colonies in the spring.

Feeding Habits: Adults feed on nectar and pollen as well as small insects which they capture to feed their young.

$\frac{3}{4}''$

BEETLES

COLEOPTERA

Nearly one third of all animals — 40 percent of all insects — are beetles. They are found everywhere except the ocean and come in a variety of colors, shapes, and sizes. They are best recognized by their hard, opaque wing covers or *elytra,* which meet in a straight line down the middle of their backs. These sheaths cover most of the thorax and abdomen, giving the beetle a completely armored appearance. A pair of membranous hind wings is intricately folded beneath. In flight, the beetle lifts its wing covers and holds them stiffly out to the sides so that the back wings can move freely. Since this is very awkward, many beetles seldom fly and some have fused wing covers so they aren't even tempted to try it. There are those, however, that possess a real enthusiasm for aerodynamics. The convergent lady beetle spends several days each fall flying to the mountains where she winters in the snow and ice.

In general, beetles have poor eyesight. They bump into things when flying and tend to get steered off course. Their sense of smell is quite good, though, and they are attracted to many of the paler, less fragrant flowers that butterflies and bees ignore.

Beetles undergo complete metamorphosis from egg to larva to pupa to adult. Eggs are laid in or on the soil, in plant debris, or on the leaves of host plants. They hatch into plump, flat or wormlike larvae called *grubs.* Grubs can be distinguished from the larvae of other insects by their well-developed heads and three pairs of legs. They pupate in cells formed in the soil or in other protected places, but they rarely build cocoons. The entire life cycle usually requires one year with some species producing up to four generations annually and still others requiring several years to produce just one.

Both larvae and adults have chewing mouthparts. With a few exceptions, they share the same diet. Some, such as lady beetles and ground beetles, are important predators of plant-eating insects. They have pointed jaws with sharp cutting edges. Beetles with hairy jaws that lack distinct teeth feed on pollen. Those with short, stout jaws are generally plant-feeders that skeletonize leaves and chew holes in flowers and fruits. Those that enter stems and roots as larvae are commonly called *borers* and are described in that chapter of this book. Beetles with mouthparts attached to the end of a cylindrical snout, burrow into plant tissue. They are discussed in the "Weevils" chapter of this book.

Although most plant-eating beetles rely on weeds for food, some species feed on cultivated plants. Usually their damage is tolerable and they are kept in check by natural enemies. Birds, toads, rodents, spiders, and many predatory and parasitic insects feed on beetle eggs, larvae, and adults. Yet, like other insects, they may get out of hand unless the gardener understands the life cycles of the creatures and employs appropriate cultural methods.

Note the overwintering habits of pestiferous beetles and eliminate their winter quarters. Cultivate during the proper season to destroy larvae and pupae in the soil. Take advantage of the beetle's natural cycle by planting during its "off-season." Cover plants with netting or cheesecloth during migration and egg-laying periods. Know the preferred foods of each species and rotate crops accordingly.

Because of their particularly strong armor, most beetles are fairly resistant to contact poisons and repellents. Pyrethrum, sabadilla dust, and a stomach poison called false hellebore are effective against some beetles but, as with any poisons, they should be used only when the insects are posing a serious threat to the crop's productivity. Try a light dust of diatomaceous earth (Perma-Guard) to kill beetles in the grub stage. Handpicking is the best and safest control in the home garden.

BEETLE
Asparagus Beetle
Crioceris asparagi

Seip / Larva

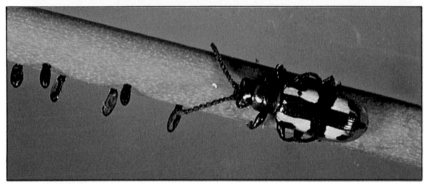

Kriner / Adult with eggs

Range: Widespread throughout North America.

Description: Metallic blue to black with four white spots and reddish margins on the wing covers, reddish thorax with two spots, bluish head; slender; ¼ inch long. EGGS: Black, shiny; laid on young spears. LARVA: Gray or greenish with black head and legs; plump; less than ⅓ inch long.

Life Cycle: Two to four generations per year. Adults overwinter in plant debris.

Host Plants: Asparagus.

Feeding Habits: Adults and larvae chew spears during spring months. In summer, they may defoliate the plants.

Insect Predators: Chalcid wasps, lady beetle larvae.

Natural Controls: Apply rotenone for serious infestations.

¼"

BEETLE
Bean Leaf Beetle
Cerotoma trifurcata

Jenkins / Adult

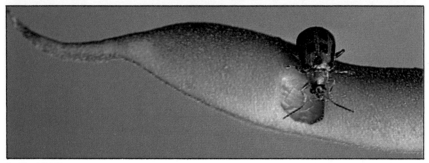

Jenkins / Adult

Range: Eastern North America, especially in the southeastern United States.

Description: Reddish orange, shiny with a black head and often with black spots; ¼ inch long. EGGS: Laid on the underside of leaves. LARVA: White, narrow grub.

Life Cycle: One or two generations per year.

Host Plants: Bean, pea, soybean.

Feeding Habits: Larvae bore into roots and nodules, sometimes girdling the stems. Adults feed on leaves throughout the summer, but controls are seldom necessary.

Natural Controls: Apply rotenone or pyrethrum if handpicking does not control the beetles.

¼"

BEETLE
Carrot Beetle
Bothynus gibbosus

Oregon / Adult

Range: Throughout most of North America, except in the Deep South.

Description: Reddish brown or black; hard shelled with fine punctures in lines on the back; ½ inch long. EGGS: Whitish, laid in the soil in early spring. LARVA: Bluish white with a brown head; curved; 1 inch long.

Similar Insects: June beetle (p. 38).

Life Cycle: One generation per year. Overwinters as an adult in the soil.

Host Plants: Beet, carrot, celery, corn, parsley, parsnip, potato.

Feeding Habits: Larvae chew roots of various grain crops. Adult beetles feed on stems and roots of host plants, but rarely do any damage.

½"

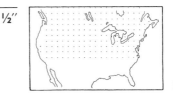

BEETLE
Colorado Potato Beetle
Leptinotarsa decemlineata

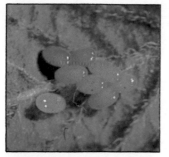

Badgley / Eggs

Jenkins / Adults

Jenkins / Larva

Range: Throughout North America, except the South.

Description: Yellow with black stripes on wing covers and dark dots just behind the head; hard shelled, very convex; 1/3 inch long. EGGS: Orange; laid in rows on underside of leaves. LARVA: Red with black legs and head, changing to pink or orange with two rows of black spots on each side; plump.

Life Cycle: One to three generations per year. Adults overwinter in the soil.

Host Plants: Eggplant, pepper, potato, tomato.

Feeding Habits: Adults and grubs feed on leaves.

Insect Predators: Ground beetle *(Harpalus caliginosus).*

Natural Controls: Mulch well with a 1-foot layer of clean hay or straw. Apply rotenone if necessary.

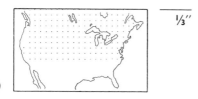

1/3″

BEETLE
Fig Beetle
Cotinis texana

Badgley / Adult

Ross / Adult

Range: Southwestern United States. The very similar green June beetle (*C. nitida*) is common in the southeastern and central states.

Description: Green or coppery with bronze wing-cover margins; very large, flat, broad; ½ inch long. EGGS: Gray; oval or round; laid in soil rich in organic matter. LARVA: Whitish with a brown head; thick; up to 2 inches long; it surfaces in wet weather and tends to crawl on its back.

Life Cycle: One generation per year. Larvae overwinter deep below the soil surface, pupate in early spring, and adults emerge in early or mid summer.

Host Plants: Most tree fruits and berries as well as corn and other vegetables.

Feeding Habits: Adults chew holes in leaves; larvae disturb roots by tunnelling or ruin them by feeding.

Natural Controls: Clear away piles of compost and grass clippings that are near the orchard.

½"

BEETLE
Flea Beetle/Striped Flea Beetle
Phyllotreta striolata

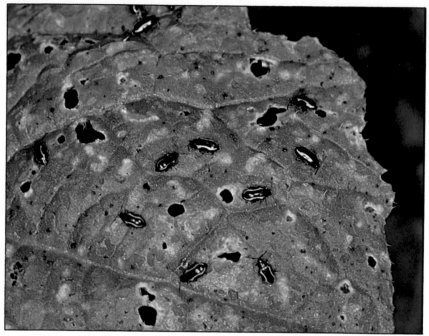

Jenkins / Adults and damage

Range: Throughout North America.

Description: Black, shiny, with curved yellow or white stripes; active, hops away when disturbed; 1/10 inch long. EGGS: Whitish; minute; laid in the soil.

Similar Insects: Grape flea beetle (p. 34).

Life Cycle: One or two generations per year. Adults overwinter in garden weeds and trash.

Host Plants: Broccoli, cabbage, cauliflower. Similar species on almost every vegetable.

Feeding Habits: Adults and larvae chew tiny holes in leaves and transmit viral and bacterial diseases.

Natural Controls: Dust with diatomaceous earth or with rotenone for serious infestations.

1/10"

BEETLE
Grape Colaspis/Clover Rootworm
Colaspis brunnea

Jenkins / Adults

Range: United States and southern Canada.

Description: Light brown; oval; ⅕ inch long. EGGS: Laid at the base of plants. LARVA: Whitish; plump.

Similar Insects: June beetle (p. 38); northern corn rootworm (p. 47); and other rootworms feeding on blueberry, cranberry, grape, strawberry.

Life Cycle: One generation per year. Larvae overwinter in the soil.

Host Plants: Apple, bean, corn, grape, melon, potato, strawberry.

Feeding Habits: Adults make long, curved, or zigzag marks in leaves, but seldom do serious damage. Larvae burrow into large roots and chew smaller ones; they may also destroy germinating seed.

Natural Controls: Thorough fall cultivation destroys larvae.

⅕"

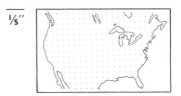

BEETLE
Grape Flea Beetle
Altica chalybea

Jenkins / Adult

Range: Eastern United States and southern Canada with similar species throughout North America.

Description: Metallic blue or green; $1/12$ inch long. EGGS: Laid in soil or on weeds. LARVA: Yellowish with black spots; minute.

Similar Insects: Striped flea beetle (p. 32).

Life Cycle: One or two generations per year. Adults hibernate in garden trash or soil.

Host Plants: Apple, grape, plum; related species feed on blueberry, strawberry.

Feeding Habits: Adults feed on youngest leaves of host plants, riddling them with shot holes. Larvae also chew on buds and leaves.

Natural Controls: Rarely necessary since plants can withstand the loss of some leaf area. If the damage is intolerable, dust with rotenone.

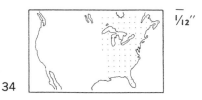

$1/12''$

Ross / Adult

Range: United States and southern Canada with many other similar species throughout North America.

Description: Blackish puple with green thorax; 1 inch long. EGGS: Whitish; laid in soil. LARVA: Yellowish gray to white; flat with sharp jaws.

Similar Insects: Rove beetles (p. 48); various tiger beetles (p. 57).

Life Cycle: One generation per year. Adults hibernate in the soil.

Feeding Habits: Adults feed at night on many soft-bodied larvae, including cankerworms and tent caterpillars.

1″

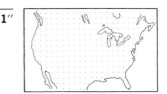

BEETLE
Ground Beetle
Carabus nemoralis

Jenkins / Larva

Oregon / Adult

Range: Northern United States and southern Canada, particularly in the West. Similar species throughout North America.

Description: Black with tinges of violet on the outer edges of the wing covers; heavily armored; long legged; nocturnal; 1 inch long. EGGS: Laid in the soil. LARVA: Whitish to light brown; elongate with large head.

Similar Insects: Fiery searcher (p. 35).

Life Cycle: One generation per year. Adults hibernate in garden trash.

Feeding Habits: Adults are fierce predators of many kinds of slugs and snails.

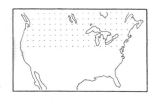

1″

BEETLE
Japanese Beetle
Popillia japonica

Ross / Adults

Range: Eastern United States, but is moving westward.

Description: Metallic blue or green with coppery wing covers; two small patches of white hair on the abdomen and five patches on each side below the wing covers; ½ inch long. EGGS: White; laid singly or in groups in sod. LARVA: Grayish white with brown head; plump; ¾ inch long.

Life Cycle: Mature grubs overwinter deep in the soil and begin to move upward in the spring. Pupation occurs in early summer. Adults feed from midsummer to fall. Eggs are laid in late summer. Life cycle is two years.

Host Plants: Apple, cherry, grape, peach, plum, quince, raspberry, rhubarb, and many others.

Feeding Habits: Adults skeletonize leaves and devour flowers. Larvae chew plant roots.

Insect Predators: Fall tiphia *(Tiphia popilliavora)*, spring tiphia wasp *(T. vernalis)*, tachinid flies *(Hyperecteina aldrichi* and *Prosena siberita).*

Natural Controls: Dust with milky spore disease (Doom) to control grubs; rotenone spray or dust controls adults.

½"

37

BEETLE
June Beetle/May Beetle/Daw Bug
Phyllophaga sp.

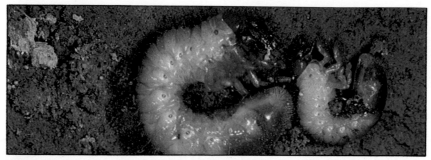

Jenkins / White grubs

Ross / Adult

Range: Various species found throughout North America.

Description: Reddish brown or black; robust, hard shelled; 1 inch long. EGGS: Laid separately several inches below soil surface. LARVA: Grayish white with brown head; plump.

Similar Insects: Grubs similar to Japanese beetle (p. 37). Adults superficially resemble carrot beetle (p. 29).

Life Cycle: One generation every three years. Grubs overwinter in soil the first two years; the third winter is spent in the pupal stage.

Host Plants: Potato, strawberry.

Feeding Habits: Grubs feed on underground plant parts during the summer. In spring, they chew roots of garden crops.

Natural Controls: Control grubs with milky spore disease (Doom).

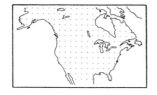

1″

BEETLE
Lady Beetles
Cycloneda sp.

Ross / *C. polita*

Gossington / *Eggs*

Gossington / *C. sanguinea and pupa*

Range: Western United States. Similar species distributed in the South and West.

Description: Orange to bright red wing covers with few or no markings, black and white marks just behind the head; $\frac{1}{10}$ to $\frac{1}{4}$ inch long. EGGS: Orange; laid upright in clusters on leaves and stems. LARVA: Grayish; flat bodied; wrinkled.

Life Cycle: Many generations per year. Overwinter as adults.

Feeding Habits: Larvae and adults eat aphids, mealybugs, and scales.

$\frac{1}{4}''$

BEETLE
Lady Beetle
Hippodamia convergens

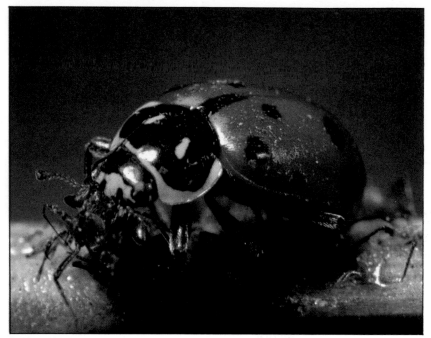

Badgley / Adult feeding on aphid

Range: Throughout North America.

Description: Orange or red, usually with 12 black spots, black pronotum with two white stripes and white rims; ¼ inch long. EGGS: Orange; cylindrical. LARVA: Black with orange spots; long, flat; ½ inch long.

Life Cycle: One generation per year. In most regions adults overwinter in garden trash; in the West, adults migrate in fall to hibernate in the mountains.

Feeding Habits: Adults and larvae are important predators of many aphids and sometimes feed on mealybugs, scales, or other small insects.

¼″

BEETLE
Lady Beetle
Olla abdominalis

Ross / Adult

Range: Throughout North America, particularly in the western United States.

Description: Gray to pale yellow with black markings; ¼ inch long. EGGS: Orange; laid on leaves and stems. LARVA: Black with yellow markings on tip of head; ½ to 1 inch long.

Life Cycle: Many generations per year. Adults overwinter in protected places.

Feeding Habits: Adults and larvae feed on many kinds of aphids.

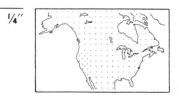

¼"

BEETLE
Lady Beetle/Spider Mite Destroyer
Stethorus picipes

Badgley / Adult

Badgley / Larva

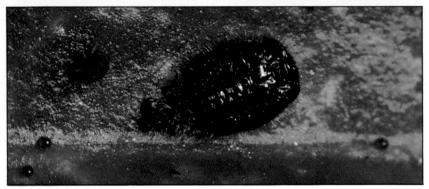

Badgley / Pupa

Range: Far West, particularly California. Similar species distributed elsewhere in North America.

Description: Black, shiny; round; $\frac{1}{30}$ inch long. EGGS: Oval; laid on leaves and bark; minute. LARVA: Dark gray to black; spined; $\frac{1}{30}$ inch long.

Life Cycle: Many generations per year. Adults overwinter in garden litter.

Feeding Habits: Adults and larvae prey on various mites.

$\frac{1}{30}''$

Badgley / Adult feeding on mealybug

Jenkins / Larva and eggs

Range: California, Florida.

Description: Red with irregular black marks; in the male, black is the predominant color. Round, convex; ¼ inch long. EGGS: Red, oval; laid singly or in small groups on the host's egg sac. LARVA: Pinkish with black markings; wrinkled, spindle shaped with many soft spines; about ⅓ inch long.

Life Cycle: Many generations each season. Overwinters as a pupa on the branches and leaves of citrus trees.

Feeding Habits: Adults and larvae prey upon cottonycushion scale and other soft-bodied insects.

¼"

43

BEETLE
Margined Blister Beetle
Epicauta pestifera

Roberts / Adult

Range: Eastern Canada, central and northern United States; an all-black species *(E. pennsylvanica)* is common in the East.

Description: Black, with a narrow gray margin around each elytra; soft bodied, elongate, with long legs and a narrow neck; ½ inch long. EGGS: Cylindrical; laid in clusters in the soil. LARVA: Vary with each instar. First instar is yellow, active, long legged. Second instar is similar but with shorter legs. Third, fourth, and fifth instars are thicker and resemble white grubs in shape. Sixth instar is darker in color and legless; the seventh instar is white, small, and very active.

Similar Insects: Striped blister beetle (p. 55).

Life Cycle: One generation per year. Beetles overwinter as partly transformed larvae in tunnels in the soil.

Host Plants: Many garden vegetables.

Feeding Habits: Swarms of adults feed on foliage and fruits. Larvae are predaceous and feed on grasshopper eggs.

Natural Controls: Wear gloves when handpicking since the insects secrete a harmful substance that may cause blisters to form.

½"

BEETLE
Mealybug Destroyer
Cryptolaemus montrouzieri

Gossington / Larva

Badgley / Adult

Range: California.

Description: Black, shiny, with reddish head, pronotum, and tip of the elytra; oval; ½ inch long. EGGS: Yellow; oval; laid singly in the egg sacs of mealybugs. LARVA: Yellow, covered with long, white waxy hairs; about ⅓ inch long.

Similar Insects: In the larval stage, it is often confused with the mealybug (pp. 181–84).

Life Cycle: There may be many generations per season. Beetles overwinter as adults.

Feeding Habits: Both larvae and adults feed on all sorts of mealybugs.

½″

45

BEETLE
Mexican Bean Beetle
Epilachna varivestis

Jenkins / Larva

Jenkins / Adult

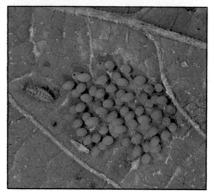

Jenkins / Eggs

Jenkins / Pupae

Range: Eastern United States and in parts of Texas, Arizona, Colorado, and Utah. Similar species with different feeding habits found throughout North America.

Description: Yellowish brown with 16 black spots on wing covers; round; ¼ inch long. EGGS: Yellow; laid in clusters on underside of leaves. LARVA: Orange; spined; ⅓ inch long.

Similar Insects: Lady beetles (pp. 39–43).

Life Cycle: One to three generations per year. Adults hibernate in open fields or woods.

Host Plants: Bean.

Feeding Habits: Larvae and adults skeletonize leaves from underneath.

Insect Predators: Various assassin bugs, a wasp *(Pediobius foveolatus)*.

Natural Controls: Apply rotenone or pyrethrum if necessary.

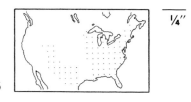

¼"

Jenkins / Adult

Range: North central United States and in isolated parts of the East and South.

Description: Bright green to yellowish green, sometimes with a brown head and pronotum; fast moving; ⅓ inch long. EGGS: Yellow; laid on the ground near corn roots. LARVA: White worm with brown head; very thin, wrinkled; up to ½ inch long.

Similar Insects: Grape colaspis (p. 33).

Life Cycle: One generation per year. Overwinters in egg stage. Larvae appear in spring, pupate in the soil in early summer, and emerge as adults in midsummer.

Host Plants: Corn, grains.

Feeding Habits: Adults chew on corn silk and eat the pollen of other plants. Larvae burrow into roots in early summer and do considerable damage.

Natural Controls: Crop rotation controls the grubs.

⅓"

BEETLE
Rove Beetles
Staphylinidae

Oregon / Adult

Range: Various species throughout North America.

Description: Brown to black, often shiny; winged or wingless with shortened elytra; slender, straight bodies with clubbed antennae and curved mouthparts; ⅛ to ½ inch long. EGGS: Laid in the soil or in decaying plant or animal material. LARVA: Similar to adults.

Similar Insects: Fiery searcher (p. 35); ground beetle (p. 36); and tiger beetle (p. 57).

Life Cycle: Several generations per year. Winter may be passed as a larva, pupa, or adult.

Feeding Habits: Most species are scavengers but some are parasitic in the larval stage. Others are predaceous and a few have a combination of these feeding habits.

½″

BEETLE
Sap Beetles
Nitidula sp.

Schuder / Adults

Range: Various species throughout North America. Other, similar sap beetles also widely distributed.

Description: Black; shiny with punctures in the wing covers; body somewhat flattened; large head; ¼ inch long. EGGS: Laid on weeds and garden plants. LARVA: White; long with spines.

Life Cycle: One generation per year. Adults hibernate in the soil.

Host Plants: Plant-eating species feed on decaying plant matter or tree sap.

Feeding Habits: Adults and larvae feed mostly on rotten fruits and garbage. Some species are predaceous on scale insects.

Natural Controls: Controls are rarely necessary, but rotenone may be used if damage is intolerable.

¼"

BEETLE
Soldier Beetle/Downy Leather-wing
Podabrus tomentosus

Oregon / Adult

Range: Most of the United States.

Description: Black with whitish thorax and head; pliable wing covers; long antennae; resembles firefly; ½ inch long. EGGS: Yellowish; laid in masses in or on soil. LARVA: Pinkish with two dark longitudinal lines on first few segments.

Life Cycle: One or two generations per year. Mature larvae overwinter in the soil.

Feeding Habits: Adults feed on aphids, so controls are unnecessary.

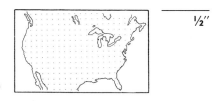

½"

Soldier Beetle/Pennsylvania Leather-wing
Chauliognathus pennsylvanicus

Moreton / Adult

Range: Eastern North America.

Description: Golden or dull orange with black markings on the wing covers, black head; soft bodied; ½ inch long. EGGS: Laid in groups in the soil. LARVA: Whitish; flattened and hairy.

Life Cycle: Two generations per year. Larvae overwinter in garden trash or the soil.

Feeding Habits: Adults feed on grasshopper eggs, cucumber beetles, and various caterpillars.

½″

BEETLE
Spotted Asparagus Beetle
Crioceris duodecimpunctata

Kriner / Adult

Range: Throughout most of North America, particularly in the East.

Description: Red or brownish with 12 black spots on the back, shiny; smooth; ⅓ inch long. EGGS: Dark brown to greenish; laid on leaves. LARVA: Orange with black head and legs; plump; ⅓ inch long.

Life Cycle: One to two generations per year. Adults overwinter in the soil.

Host Plants: Asparagus.

Feeding Habits: Adults feed on spears and leaves in early summer. Larvae do little damage.

Insect Predators: Chalcid wasps.

Natural Controls: Apply rotenone.

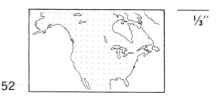

⅓"

BEETLE
Spotted Cucumber Beetle
Diabrotica undecimpunctata howardi

Ross / Adult

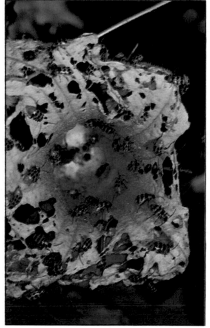

Jenkins / Damage

Range: Southern Canada and the eastern United States; a similar species is found in the West.

Description: Greenish yellow with a small black head and 11 black spots on the back; ¼ inch long. EGGS: Yellow; oval; laid in the soil at the base of plants. LARVA: Beige with a brown head and brown spot on the last body segment; about ½ inch long.

Life Cycle: In the North, there are one or two generations; in the South, there are up to four. Adult overwinters in plant debris and garden trash.

Host Plants: Corn, cucumber, eggplant, melon, pea, potato, squash, and tomato, as well as many tree fruits.

Feeding Habits: Adults chew holes in plant leaves, flowers, and fruits, and transmit brown rot among stone fruits. Larvae eat roots and stems of plants early in the season.

Insect Predators: A tachinid fly *(Celatoria diabrotica).*

Natural Controls: Use rotenone or pyrethrum for serious infestations.

¼″

BEETLE
Spotted Grapevine Beetle
Pelidnota punctata

Carr / Adult

Range: Eastern United States.

Description: Reddish brown or tan with black spots around the margins of the wing covers; broad, robust; 1 inch long. LARVA: Tan; found in decaying tree stumps and roots.

Life Cycle: One generation per year. Beetle overwinters in the larval stage.

Host Plants: Grape.

Feeding Habits: Larvae feed on plant roots. Adults may chew foliage and fruit, but damage is minor and controls are unnecessary.

1″

BEETLE
Striped Blister Beetle
Epicauta vittata

Jenkins / Adult

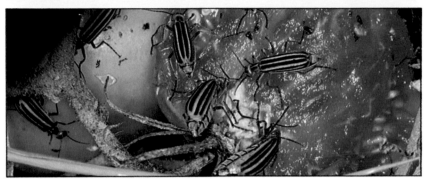

Jenkins / Damage

Range: Eastern North America and the central United States.

Description: Yellow with black stripes, black striped head, black legs; ½ inch long. EGGS: Cylindrical, laid in shallow cells in the soil. LARVA: Yellowish to white with later instars much darker.

Similar Insects: Margined blister beetle (p. 44).

Life Cycle: One generation per year. Larvae overwinter in the soil.

Host Plants: Bean, beet, melon, pea, potato, tomato, and other vegetable plants.

Feeding Habits: Larvae feed on grasshopper eggs. Adults feed on foliage and fruits.

Natural Controls: Wear gloves when handpicking since the insects secrete a harmful substance that may cause blisters to form.

½″

BEETLE
Striped Cucumber Beetle
Acalymma vittata

Kriner / Adult

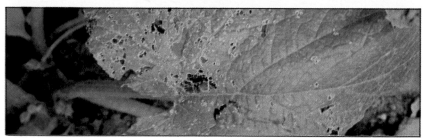
Kriner / Damage

Range: Eastern North America.

Description: Pale yellow to orange with three black stripes and black head; ¼ inch long. EGGS: Orange, laid in the soil at the base of host plants. LARVA: White; slender; ¼ inch long.

Life Cycle: One generation in the North; two to four in the South. Adults overwinter in plant debris.

Host Plants: Bean, corn, cucumber, melon, pea, pumpkin, squash.

Feeding Habits: Adults chew leaves and flowers and transmit bacterial wilt and cucumber mosiac. Larvae feed on underground stems and roots.

Insect Predators: Various soldier beetles.

Natural Controls: Cover plants with cheesecloth. Use rotenone dusts or sprays for serious infestations.

¼"

56

BEETLE
Tiger Beetle
Tetracha virginica

Gossington / Adult

Range: Western North America. Similar species in the South and others throughout North America.

Description: Dark bluish green or black, shiny, often with yellow markings on wings or head and thorax; long legged; strong fliers; ½ to 1 inch long. EGGS: Laid singly in burrows in the soil. LARVA: White; S-shaped with heavy spines and a hump with curved hooks in the middle of the body.

Life Cycle: Entire life cycle requires two to three years. Adults and larvae overwinter in the soil.

Feeding Habits: Adults and larvae feed during the day on many plant-eating insects.

1″

BEETLE
Whitefringed Beetle
Graphognathus leucoloma

Jenkins / Larvae and pupae

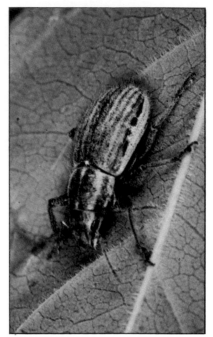

Jenkins / Adult

Range: Southeastern United States.

Description: Brownish gray with short, white hairs covering the back; short snout; cannot fly; ½ inch long. EGGS: Covered with a sticky substance; laid in masses at the base of plants. LARVA: Yellowish white; legless; about ½ inch long.

Life Cycle: One generation per year. Usually hibernates as larva in the soil, but sometimes as egg.

Host Plants: Any garden crop, particularly corn, peanut, and potato.

Feeding Habits: Adults collect on leaves and feed inward from the margins. Larvae chew on the outer root tissues and may sever the main root.

Natural Controls: Clean cultivation is the only effective organic control measure.

½"

BORERS

LEPIDOPTERA AND COLEOPTERA

Caterpillars or beetle grubs that feed within stems, branches, or roots are known as borers. Representing the larval stage of many different insect families, they feed on a variety of garden crops, small fruits, and orchard trees. Adult members of this group lay eggs on the surface of plants or thrust them into plant tissue. A few species deposit eggs in the soil. Upon hatching, these larvae chew their way through roots and stems or tunnel into the inner bark of trees. For information on their life cycles, see the "Beetles" and "Caterpillars" chapters of this book (pp. 25–58 and 93–139).

Since they spend most of their lives within the plant, borers may do considerable damage before they are discovered. Orchard trees can become stunted and produce deformed fruits. A waxy or sticky sawdustlike substance may exude from holes in the bark. Infested vegetable plants wilt suddenly and masses of greenish excrement appear near the entrance holes in the stems.

All plants are vulnerable to borer injury, particularly those that are ailing or weak. Trees injured by ice, wind, fire, or even by overly zealous lawn mowers, are very susceptible to infestation. Drought invites borers, especially when the tree's roots become very dry.

The best way to protect trees in the face of these problems is to keep them well watered and fertilized. Wrap strips of burlap, sticky paper, or corrugated cardboard around the trunks to thwart the march of crawling insects.Use proper pruning techniques to remove injured or weak branches of trees. Examine bark carefully for entrance holes or stained areas and check the base of the trees several inches below the soil surface for brown castings.

Unfortunately, once borers have set up housekeeping inside the tree, very little can be done to eliminate them. If only a few are present, they can be killed by probing their holes with a flexible wire or the tip of a knife. Remove and burn all infested branches in the spring, before the adults emerge to lay more eggs.

Like fruit trees, garden crops and small fruits can be severely damaged by borers unless the problem is recognized early in the season. Plants are most likely to be injured if set out too early in the season or if the garden has not been thoroughly cultivated and cleaned. Spade the soil deeply each spring to eliminate overwintering insects and to destroy eggs. Rotate crops and juggle planting times so that crops mature after the borers have finished feeding. Destroy all vines and plant debris immediately after harvest.

If sudden wilting occurs, cut and destroy the infested stems immediately. Sometimes the grub can be removed without killing the entire plant. Slit the stem just above the entrance hole, kill the borer with a knife, then bind the stem together or cover it with soil so that new roots may form.

Poisons and repellents have little effect on borers unless they are applied when the beetles and moths are laying eggs or just as the larvae hatch and enter the plant. Contact insecticides such as rotenone or pyrethrum dusts are sometimes effective during these periods. However, woodpeckers, crows, king-birds, vireos, ants, predatory beetles, and many wasps destroy far more borers than any dust can.

BORER
European Corn Borer
Ostrinia nubilalis

Jenkins / Pupae

Kriner / Eggs

Badgley / Larva

Jenkins / Adult

Range: Northern and central United States and southern Canada.

Description: Grayish pink caterpillar with dark head and spots on the top of each segment; 1 inch long. ADULT: Yellowish brown moth with dark bands on the wings; nocturnal; 1-inch wingspan. EGGS: White; laid in masses on the underside of leaves.

Similar Insects: Corn earworm (p. 101).

Life Cycle: One to three generations per year. Larvae hibernate in stalks.

Host Plants: Corn, also many garden crops.

Feeding Habits: Young larvae chew leaves and tassels of corn and may feed on other plants. Later, they bore into stalks and ears and the stems of garden crops.

Insect Predators: Braconid wasp *(Macrocentrus grandi)*, tachinid fly *(Lydella stabulans grisescens)*.

Natural Controls: Split stalks below entrance holes and remove borers.

1″

BORER
Flatheaded Appletree Borer
Chrysobothris femorata

Schuder / Adult

Range: Common throughout North America, particularly the East.

Description: Yellow to white grub with a broad, flat area just behind the head; usually curved; 1¼ inches long. ADULT: Grayish brown, shiny beetle; blunt head; ½ inch long. EGGS: Laid in cracks in the bark.

Life Cycle: One generation per year. Overwinters as a grub in the bark. Pupation occurs in early spring.

Host Plants: Apple, apricot, cherry, currant, peach, pear, pecan, plum, and raspberry.

Feeding Habits: Borer enters bark and feeds there until full grown when it mines deeper into the wood. Overlaying bark is stained, but no castings appear. Vigorous trees are not harmed, but young transplants may be killed.

1¼″

Grape Root Borer
Vitacea polistiformis

Jenkins / Larva

Jenkins / Adult

Range: Throughout North America.

Description: Whitish, round caterpillar; 1¾ inches long. ADULT: Brown and orange, clear-winged moth. EGGS: Laid on foliage.

Life Cycle: One generation per year with up to two years required to complete the life cycle. Pupae overwinter in the soil.

Host Plants: Grape.

Feeding Habits: Larvae feed within roots, remain there for two years.

Natural Controls: Cultivation of the soil is the best control.

1¾″

BORER
Lesser Peachtree Borer/Plumtree Borer
Synanthedon pictipes

Kriner / Larva

Range: Southern and eastern United States; similar species throughout North America.

Description: Pale yellow or white caterpillar with brown head; 1 inch long. ADULT: Metallic blue, clear-winged moth with yellow marks; wasplike; 1⅓ inches long. EGGS: Laid in bark crevices.

Similar Insects: Peachtree borer (p. 66).

Life Cycle: One generation per year. Larva hibernates in burrow or just below the soil surface. Pupation takes place within the burrow, but a silk web can be seen at the opening.

Host Plants: Apricot, cherry, peach.

Feeding Habits: Borers work on injured trunks and limbs. Masses of gummy sawdust ooze from holes in upper trunk and branches.

Natural Controls: Each spring, surround trees with a ring of tobacco dust about 2 inches wide. Trap moths with a sticky material such as Tanglefoot or Stikem applied to the lower trunk and branches.

1″

BORER
Limabean Pod Borer
Etiella zinckenella

Badgley / Adult

Badgley / Larva

Range: Throughout North America, particularly in California.

Description: Pink, tan, or greenish caterpillar; ½ inch long. ADULT: Gray moth with orange and white bands across the wing; strong flier; 1-inch wingspan. EGGS: White; elliptical; laid in pods.

Life Cycle: Two to four generations per year. Hibernates as a pupa in the soil.

Host Plants: All beans, peas.

Feeding Habits: Larvae bore into the pod to feed, leaving no trace of entrance. When mature, they chew holes in pods and fall to the ground to pupate.

Natural Controls: Handpicking is usually sufficient.

½"

65

BORER
Peachtree Borer
Synanthedon exitiosa

Ross / Adult

Kriner / Larva and pupa

Range: Throughout North America.

Description: Pale yellow or whitish caterpillar with brown head; 1 inch long. ADULT: Steel blue, clear-winged moth with yellow stripes (male) or a wide orange band (female) around the abdomen. EGGS: Brown or gray; laid in small groups near the base of trees.

Similar Insects: Codling moth (p. 100); lesser peachtree borer (p. 64); oriental fruit moth (p. 124).

Life Cycle: One generation per year. Larva passes winter in its burrow and pupates in a brown cocoon in the soil each spring.

Host Plants: Apricot, cherry, peach, plum.

Feeding Habits: Borers chew inner bark of lower tree trunk; a mass of gummy sawdust appears at the base of injured trees. Vectors of wilt fungus.

Natural Controls: Each spring, surround base of trees with a ring of tobacco dust 2 inches wide.

1″

Jenkins / Adult

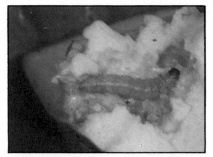
Jenkins / Larva

Jenkins / Pupa

Range: Southeastern United States. Sometimes found north to New York and west to Nebraska.

Description: Yellowish white caterpillar with dark spots when young; older larva greenish with brown head; ¾ inch long. ADULT: Yellowish white to tan moth; slender body; long hairy scales on tip of abdomen; 1¼-inch wingspan. EGGS: White; minute; laid singly or in small groups on buds, leaves, stalks, and fruits.

Life Cycle: One to four broods per year. Hibernates as pupa within a rolled leaf. Adult emerges in late spring.

Host Plants: Cucumber, melon, pumpkin, squash.

Feeding Habits: Larvae enter developing buds and fruits. Each worm may enter several.

Natural Controls: Slit infested stems and remove the borers, then heap dirt over the injured stem to encourage rooting.

¾″

BORER
Potato Stalk Borer
Trichobaris trinotata

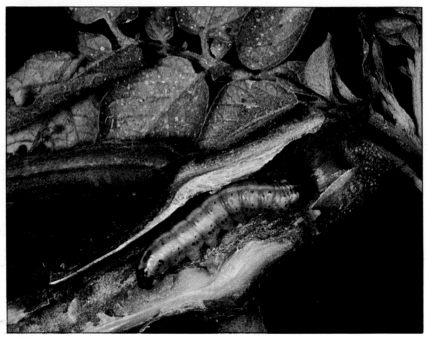

Kriner / Larva

Range: Throughout most of North America, except the Far West.

Description: Yellowish white grub with brown head; ⅓ inch long. ADULT: Bluish black weevil covered with fine gray hairs and marked with three black spots at the base of the wing covers; ⅒ to ⅕ inch long. EGGS: Deposited singly in holes within stems and petioles.

Life Cycle: One generation per year. Overwinters as an adult in garden trash.

Host Plants: Eggplant, ground-cherry, potato, tomato.

Feeding Habits: Borers hollow out the stems of plants causing them to wilt and die. In spring, adults chew holes in stems.

Natural Controls: Slit infested stalks and remove the borers, then cover injured stems with earth.

⅓"

BORER
Potato Tuberworm
Phthorimaea operculella

Badgley / Adult

Badgley / Larva in leaf

Badgley / Larva in stem

Range: Southern United States from Florida to California.

Description: Pinkish white with a brown head; wormlike; ½ inch long. ADULT: Grayish brown moth marked with darker brown; very narrow wings; ½-inch wingspan. EGGS: Laid singly or in groups on the underside of leaves or in the eyes of tubers.

Life Cycle: Up to six generations per year. Larva pupates in tubers and over-winters in garden trash.

Host Plants: Eggplant, tomato.

Feeding Habits: Larvae tunnel into stems and make silk-lined burrows in the tubers.

Natural Controls: Clip and destroy infested vines.

½″

BORER
Raspberry Crown Borer
Pennisetia marginata

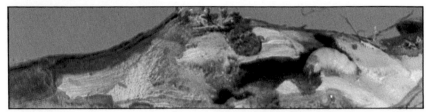

Oregon / Larva

Oregon / Adult

Range: Northern United States and southern Canada.

Description: White caterpillar; ½ inch long. ADULT: Black, clear-winged moth with four yellow bands across the body; 1½ inches long. EGGS: Reddish brown; oval.

Similar Insects: Strawberry crown moth (p. 132).

Life Cycle: One generation per year. Larva hibernates in the bark at the base of plants.

Host Plants: Blackberry, boysenberry, raspberry.

Feeding Habits: Borers feed in the crowns and bases of canes, causing plants to wilt. Extensive galleries are made and eventually the entire canes are hollowed.

Natural Controls: Remove and destroy infested crowns in early spring or fall.

½″

BORER
Roundheaded Appletree Borer
Saperda candida

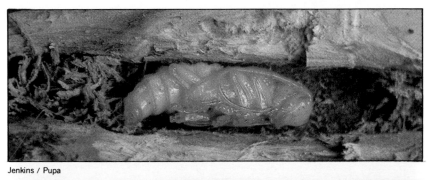

Jenkins / Pupa

Ross / Larva

Range: Eastern North America, westward to Texas.

Description: Brownish white grub with brown head; rounded, thick area behind head; 1½ inches long. ADULT: Tan or brown beetle with two white stripes and white head, white underside; 1 inch long. EGGS: Laid in curved slits in the bark.

Life Cycle: Two to four years required to complete the life cycle. Larva hibernates in its feeding position. Pupation occurs in spring and beetle emerges in early to mid summer.

Host Plants: Apple, peach, plum, quince.

Feeding Habits: The first year, borers feed on the bark, producing dark brown stains. During the next one or two seasons, they enter the inner bark, sending out a brownish frass. The last year, they mine the heartwood. Adults may feed on foliage or fruits.

Natural Controls: To kill the grubs, pour boiling water into the entrance holes.

1½″

BORER
Shothole Borer/Fruittree Bark Borer
Scolytus rugulosus

Oregon / Adult

Oregon / Larva

Clemson / Damage

Range: Throughout North America.

Description: White grub with reddish head; ⅛ inch long. ADULT: Dark brown or black beetle with red wing tips; ¹/₁₀ inch long. EGGS: Laid in galleries made parallel to the bark grain.

Life Cycle: One to three broods per year. Borers overwinter in inner bark.

Host Plants: Almond, apple, apricot, cherry, peach, pear, plum, quince.

Feeding Habits: Adults drill small, round entrance and exit holes in bark. Adults and larvae feed in inner bark, making centipede-shaped galleries.

Natural Controls: Whitewash lower trunk and branches during egg laying.

⅛″

BORER
Southwestern Corn Borer
Diatraea grandiosella

Jenkins / Adult

Jenkins / Older larva

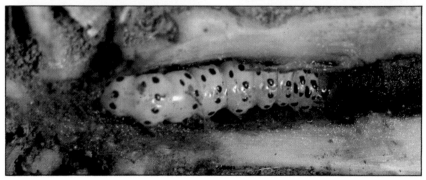

Jenkins / Young larva

Range: Southwestern United States with similar species found elsewhere.

Description: Grayish white caterpillar with dark brown spots that disappear in winter; 1 inch long. ADULT: Tan to yellowish moth; 1¼-inch wingspan. EGGS: White to reddish brown; flat; laid in overlapping rows on the underside of leaves.

Life Cycle: Two generations. Larva overwinters in plant roots. Pupation occurs in early spring.

Host Plants: Corn.

Feeding Habits: Young borers feed on leaves, cut holes in stalks, and pupate there. Second-generation larvae feed within stalks and tunnel into roots where they hibernate.

Natural Controls: Remove stubble and refuse after harvesting corn; cultivate the soil in late fall.

1″

BORER
Squash Vine Borer
Melittia satyriniformis

Kriner / Damage

Visual Teaching / Adult

Kriner / Larva

Range: East of the Rocky Mountains, in United States and southern Canada.

Description: White caterpillar with a brown head; wrinkled; 1 inch long. ADULT: Orange and black, clear-winged moth with coppery fore wings and black stripes around the abdomen; 1 to 1½ inches long. EGGS: Brown; flat, oval; laid singly along the stems.

Life Cycle: One to two generations. Hibernates as larva or pupa in a cocoon, 1 inch deep in the soil.

Host Plants: Cucumber, gourd, melon, pumpkin, squash.

Feeding Habits: Borers enter base of stems in early summer, causing vines to wilt suddenly and masses of greenish frass to exude from holes in the stems.

Natural Controls: Slit the stem, remove the borer, and heap dirt over the damaged stalk.

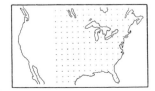

1"

BUGS

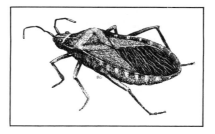

HEMIPTERA

To most of us, a bug that is not a concealed microphone or a flu germ is any sort of six-legged creature. In entomological terms, however, true bugs are only those insects belonging to the order Hemiptera. They range in size from tiny specks that can be seen only with the aid of a magnifying glass, to large ones almost as big as your thumb. Their fore wings are thickened and leathery at the base with membranous tips that overlap when the insect is at rest. The front of the thorax is usually very large and distinctly separate from the rest of the thorax, which forms a triangular area called the *scutellum.* All true bugs are marked with this triangle and can be recognized at a glance. The only insects that are similarly marked are leafhoppers and cicadas (Homoptera), but their wings are usually entirely membranous and do not lie flat against the body.

Bugs have incomplete metamorphosis in which development occurs in three stages. Eggs hatch into small, wingless nymphs that, to varying degrees, resemble the adult form. Through a series of molts, these young gradually increase in size and, when almost mature, they develop wings. The life cycle may take several weeks or an entire year. Most of the garden species hibernate as adults, but some pass the winter in the egg or nymph stage.

Mouthparts are enclosed in a beak that arises on the front part of the insect's head and curves beneath the body. In some bugs, the tip of the beak rests in a groove and the insect moves it back and forth to make a high-pitched squeaking sound.

Most true bugs are plant-eaters with diets unacceptable to man. In feeding, they pierce the epidermis of the leaf with their beaks, inject salivary fluids into the tissue, and draw out the partly digested cell sap. This causes leaves to develop small, sunken spots and bleached areas. If enough bugs are present, leaves may wilt and die. Fruits, tender twigs, and flowers of most garden plants and orchard trees may also be injured by bugs. Some species, such as the squash bug, inject a toxic fluid into their hosts, causing them to wilt suddenly and die.

Garden sanitation and weed control are the best ways to prevent the growth of large populations of plant-eating bugs. Certain insecticides such as nicotine leached from tobacco leaves, pyrethrum, rotenone, sabadilla, and ryania may help control bugs when they are truly damaging garden crops.

There are many species of true bugs that eat other insects instead of plants. Small, brown, soft-bodied damsel bugs feed on aphids, leafhoppers, and small caterpillars. The oddly shaped ambush bugs catch insects with their toothed front legs. Various assassin bugs and predaceous stink bugs attack caterpillars, beetle grubs, and mites.

BUG
Apple Red Bug
Lygidea mendax

Heilman / Damage   Kriner / Nymph

Range: Eastern United States.

Description: Bright red with brownish midsections and black legs; a related species is covered with long white hairs; ⅓ inch long. EGGS: Laid on bark.

Similar Insects: Tarnished plant bug (p. 91).

Life Cycle: One generation per year. Eggs remain on the limbs throughout the winter and hatch just before blossoms open.

Host Plants: Apple.

Feeding Habits: Nymphs and adults make small holes in leaves and feed on developing fruit. Affected apples are gnarled.

Natural Controls: Apply dormant-oil spray just as nymphs emerge.

⅓″

Ross / Adult

Moreton / Nymph

Range: Various species found throughout North America.

Description: Brown or black; flat, sculptured body with a groove that holds the stout beak when at rest; abdomen may flare outward beneath the wings; often with peculiar hood or structure behind the head; ½ inch long. EGGS: Usually laid in the soil. NYMPH: Often brightly colored.

Life Cycle: Various species have different life cycles and habits. In most cases, just one generation occurs each year with the complete cycle sometimes requiring several years. Some hibernate as nymphs or adults, others pass the winter as eggs.

Feeding Habits: Adults and nymphs feed on larval and occasionally on adult forms of many plant-eating insects.

½″

BUG
Bigeyed Bug
Geocoris pallens

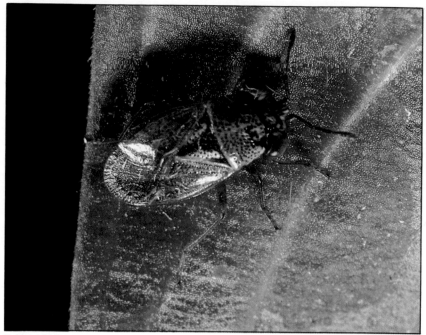

Badgley / Adult

Range: Western North America.

Description: Buff to gray with tiny black spots on the head and thorax; very large eyes; ¼ inch long. EGGS: Whitish gray with red spots; football shaped.

Life Cycle: Several generations per year. Adults hibernate in garden trash.

Feeding Habits: Both adults and nymphs feed on aphids, blister beetles, immature bugs, leafhoppers, and spider mites.

¼"

BUG
Boxelder Bug
Leptocoris trivittatus

Ross / Adult

Range: Throughout North America.

Description: Grayish brown to black with red stripes on the thorax and thin diagonal red lines on the upper part of the wings; ½ inch long. EGGS: Laid on bark and leaves. NYMPH: Bright red.

Life Cycle: One to two broods per year. Adult females hibernate in sheltered spots.

Host Plants: Usually boxelder, but bugs may also feed on various fruit trees.

Feeding Habits: Bugs feed on foliage and flowers of ornamentals but sometimes infest orchard crops. Fruits may be punctured and slightly deformed, but the injury is usually minimal.

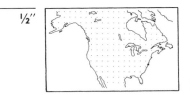

½″

BUG
Brown Stink Bug
Euschistus servus

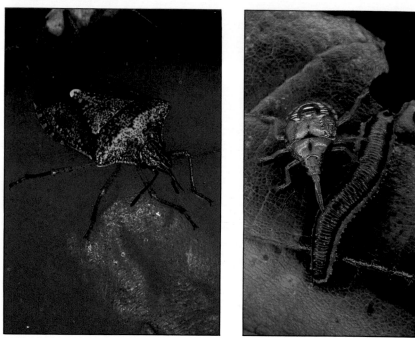

Jenkins / Adult

Moreton / Predatory nymph

Range: Eastern United States with similar species in the West and in Canada.

Description: Brown with a checked border beneath the wing covers; shield shaped; ½ inch long. EGGS: Laid on leaves and fruits.

Life Cycle: One generation per year. Hibernates in the adult or egg stages.

Host Plants: Blackberry, cabbage, corn, peach, tomato.

Feeding Habits: Adults and nymphs puncture fruit skin, causing a gummy substance to appear. Injured fruit has a catfaced or pitted appearance. Many similar stink bugs are predaceous.

Natural Controls: Weed control is the best preventative measure.

½"

BUG
Chinch Bug
Blissus leucopterus

Jenkins / Adults feeding

Heilman / Adult

Range: Eastern North America.

Description: Black with white or brown fore wings, brown legs, and brown antennae; emits an offensive odor when crushed; $\frac{1}{16}$ inch long. EGGS: White to dark red; curved; laid in the soil or on roots. NYMPH: Red with white stripe across the back or black with white spots.

Life Cycle: Two to three generations per year. Adults hibernate in clumps of grass.

Host Plants: Corn.

Feeding Habits: Nymphs and adults feed on corn leaves and stalks.

Natural Controls: Turn up a ridge of earth around the stalks and pour creosote on top.

$\frac{1}{16}''$

81

BUG
Eggplant Lace Bug
Gargaphia solani

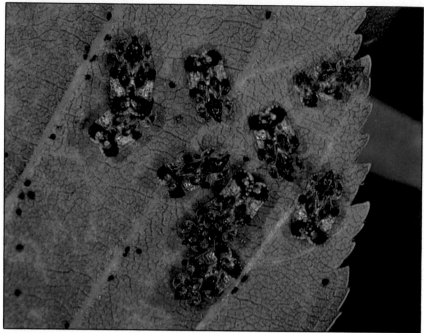

Jenkins / Adults

Range: Southern United States.

Description: Brown with a transparent, lacelike hood and covering on the wings; ¼ inch long. EGGS: Black; glued in groups to the underside of leaves. NYMPH: Brown or black; spined; without the lacelike covering.

Life Cycle: Usually one to two generations per year. Adults overwinter in garden trash.

Host Plants: Eggplant, potato, tomato.

Feeding Habits: Nymphs and adults feed on the underside of leaves, causing them to curl and turn pale. Damage is usually minimal, however.

¼″

BUG
Fourlined Plant Bug
Poecilocapsus lineatus

Carr / Adult

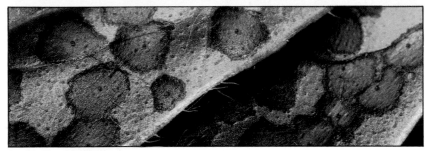

Carr / Damage

Range: Eastern North America.

Description: Yellowish green with four black stripes on the wing covers; oval; ⅓ inch long. EGGS: White; narrow; deposited in slits in stems. NYMPH: Bright orange with black dots on the thorax.

Life Cycle: One generation per year. Overwinters in the egg stage.

Host Plants: Currant, gooseberry, mint.

Feeding Habits: In early summer, nymphs and adults feed on leaves, causing spots to form. Leaves may turn brown and fall, but plants can tolerate the damage.

⅓″

BUG
Harlequin Bug/Calico Bug
Murgantia histrionica

Ross / Adult

Roberts / Eggs

Range: Southern United States.

Description: Red and black, shiny; flat, shield shaped; ¼ inch long. EGGS: White with black rings; barrel shaped; laid in double rows on the underside of leaves. NYMPH: Red and black; oval.

Life Cycle: Three to four generations per year, but in the South, it may breed year-round. Adults hibernate in plant debris and litter.

Host Plants: Brussels sprouts, cauliflower, cherry, citrus, collard, horseradish, kohlrabi, mustard, radish, turnip.

Feeding Habits: Nymphs and adults cause white and yellow blotches to appear on leaves.

Natural Controls: Dust or spray with pyrethrum or sabadilla if the problem is serious.

¼"

BUG
Leaffooted Bug
Leptoglossus phyllopus

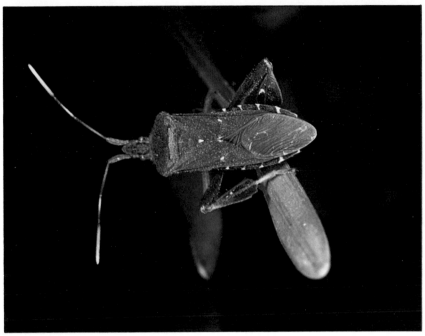

Moreton / Adult

Range: Southern United States, except in the Far West.

Description: Dark brown with a yellow band across the body; hind legs flattened like a leaf; ¾ inch long. EGGS: White; key shaped; laid on the underside of leaves.

Life Cycle: One brood per year. Adults pass the winter in sheltered locations.

Host Plants: Bean, orange, pea, peach, pecan, potato, tomato.

Feeding Habits: Adults and nymphs chew foliage and fruits.

Natural Controls: Apply sabadilla dust or pyrethrum to foliage if the damage is intolerable.

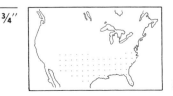

¾"

85

BUG
Minute Pirate Bug/Insidious Flower Bug
Orius sp.

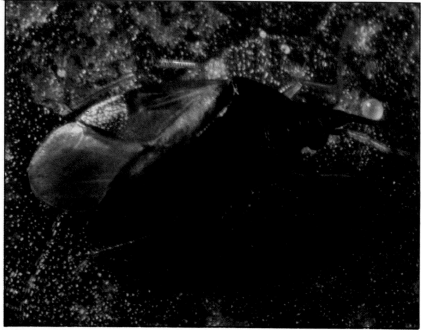

Badgley / Adult

Range: Various species throughout North America.

Description: Black and white or brownish; flat; active; $1/20$ inch long. EGGS: White or clear; laid in plant tissue.

Life Cycle: Three to four generations per year.

Feeding Habits: Adults and nymphs prey on aphids, spider mites, and thrips.

$\overline{1/20}''$

BUG
Negro Bug
Corimelaena pulicaria

Jenkins / Adults

Range: Throughout North America.

Description: Black, shiny; domed; ¹/₁₀ to ⅕ inch long. EGGS: Laid singly on leaves.

Life Cycle: Several generations per year. Adults spend the winter in garden trash.

Host Plants: Blackberry, blueberry, celery, raspberry.

Feeding Habits: Bugs feed in large groups on foliage and fruits, often lending a bad flavor to raspberries and blackberries.

⅕″

BUG
Say Stink Bug
Chlorochroa sayi

Ross / Adult   Clemson / Damage

Range: Western United States; similar species throughout North America.

Description: Bright green with three orange spots at the top of the scutellum and a whitish dot at the tip of the abdomen; ½ inch long. EGGS: Pale green or brownish; laid in groups on leaves of host plants.

Life Cycle: Several generations per year. Adults hibernate in garden trash.

Host Plants: Asparagus, bean, pea, potato.

Feeding Habits: Feeding adults and nymphs cause pods to become pimpled or misshapen and shoots to wilt.

Natural Controls: If the bugs become a serious problem, dust with sabadilla.

½″

BUG
Southern Green Stink Bug
Nezara viridula

Roberts / Damaged pecan (above)

Maslowski / Adult

Range: Southeastern United States.

Description: Light green, speckled; hibernating form may be pinkish; ½ inch long. EGGS: Glued to leaves. NYMPH: Bluish gray with red marks; round.

Similar Insects: Say stink bug (p. 88).

Life Cycle: Four to five generations per year. Adults hibernate in garden trash.

Host Plants: Bean, citrus, peach, pecan, potato, tomato.

Feeding Habits: Bugs feed on leaves and fruits, causing pods to drop prematurely and nuts to develop black pits.

Natural Controls: If the damage is intolerable, dust with sabadilla.

½″

BUG
Squash Bug
Anasa tristis

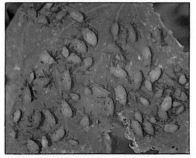

Jenkins / Adults feeding

Ross / Adult

Jenkins / Eggs hatching

Range: Throughout North America.

Description: Dark brown to black with orange or brown abdominal perimeter; emits a peculiar odor when crushed; ½ inch long. EGGS: Brown, shiny; laid in groups or singly on the underside of leaves and stems. NYMPH: Yellowish green with dark abdomen and thorax.

Life Cycle: One generation per year. Hibernates as an adult.

Host Plants: Cucumber, melon, pumpkin, squash.

Feeding Habits: Adults and nymphs congregate on leaves, causing them to wilt and blacken.

Insect Predators: The tachinid fly *(Trichopoda pennipes).*

Natural Controls: Dust with sabadilla if necessary.

½"

Tarnished Plant Bug
Lygus lineolaris

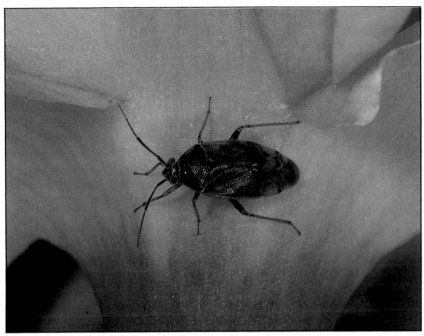

Jenkins / Adult

Range: Throughout North America.

Description: Greenish yellow to brown with yellow, brown, and black markings; yellow triangle at the end of each fore wing; ¼ inch long. EGGS: Elongate, curved; inserted in stems, tips, and leaves. NYMPH: Pale yellow.

Life Cycle: Three to five generations per year. Overwinters as an adult or nymph in garden trash.

Host Plants: Most fruits and vegetables.

Feeding Habits: Nymphs and adults suck on stem tips, buds, and fruits. They inject a toxin which deforms roots, blackens terminal shoots, dwarfs and pits fruits, and ruins flowers.

Natural Controls: Apply sabadilla dust to serious infestations.

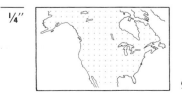

¼″

CATERPILLARS

LEPIDOPTERA

Caterpillars represent the larval stage of butterflies and moths. They are segmented and wormlike but their heads are quite distinct. They have 12 simple eyes, a pair of very short antennae, and usually six well-developed legs. In addition, caterpillars possess two to five pairs of short, hooked projections that resemble plump legs. These false legs are *prolegs*, used in walking and clinging to plants. Since they occur in almost all caterpillars and in only a few other larvae, they help distinguish caterpillars from other insects. Although sawfly larvae have prolegs, they have more than five pairs. Beetle grubs, bee and wasp larvae, and wireworms have none.

Caterpillars breathe through pores in the abdomen. Their respiratory, circulatory, and nervous systems are fundamentally the same as those of adult moths and butterflies. With only simple eyes, they can detect light but not images and must wander about in a foggy world. Having no ears, they detect sound vibrations through the fine hairs and spines that cover their bodies.

The life cycle of these rather dull creatures can almost be described as one continuous meal. All species are plant-eaters and it is believed that they rely on an acute sense of smell to seek out their favorite foods. They have chewing mouthparts of varying degrees of strength. Small larvae usually mine between the delicate surfaces of leaves or eat around the veins. Larger caterpillars feed on leaf edges, gradually moving toward the center and consuming all but the largest veins. A few bore into fruits and flowers. Those that drill into wood or feed within roots and stems are listed in the "Borers" chapter of this book.

After feeding for several weeks and molting many times, caterpillars begin to grow restless. Usually they wander about searching for comfortable places to pupate. Even if they have been feeding together, usually the larvae pupate alone. Each one selects a resting place and, spinning silk from its mouth, makes a little hook on the branch or leaf or stem. It attaches itself, hanging upside down or simply resting on the plant surface. Some caterpillars continue spinning silk until they are entirely covered by protective *cocoons.* Others, particularly butterflies, have naked pupae so you can actually watch much of the final molt as it occurs.

As soon as the caterpillar has attached itself to the stem or branch, it begins to change its form. The body is contracted or curled into a J-shape. The skin hardens, then splits and is pushed off the body, revealing a tubular pupa or *chrysalis.* This hardens and remains on the plant until the final molt.

The pupa itself is not a case or shell, but a living organism, as much alive as the original caterpillar or the butterfly or moth it will become. Whether enclosed in a cocoon or exposed to the elements, it continually produces heat and absorbs oxygen. The circulation, breathing, and, to some extent, nervous system continue to function and keep the insect alive as its body changes. 93

With the help of hormones and enzymes, the various larval structures such as prolegs and simple eyes and chewing mouthparts are altered or broken down. Adult features such as wings, mouthparts, and compound eyes are formed from the blood, fat, and tissue of the larval muscles.

If the pupa is encased in a cocoon, these changes are virtually invisible. Sometimes, however, the process can be observed through the translucent case of the chrysalis. The chrysalis may change color and it is sometimes possible to see wings forming within.

When development is complete, the insect splits its pupal shell and emerges. Its exoskeleton hardens and its long sucking tube or proboscis uncoils. The wings, damp and sticky sacs, gradually expand and flatten. These wings are covered with thousands of tiny scales overlapping like roof tiles. The bodies are also covered with scales, but these are much longer and resemble hairs.

These delicate fliers are perhaps the most refined and appealing of insects. Having eaten continuously during their lowly lives as caterpillars, they now feed entirely on nectar and water. Some species, such as silk moths, are incapable of eating, existing solely on the food stored from their larval days.

Butterflies and *moths* have incredible taste senses located on the soles of their feet. As soon as they land on a particularly sweet flower petal, they detect the nectar and their proboscis uncoils. They use their antennae to smell plants and to pick up the scent of a mate. Their compound eyes are very large, giving some species excellent vision.

Walking is fairly difficult since the insects have such large wings and a long body to balance on very small legs. Most of their movement is by flying on wings coupled together as one surface. Moths, recognized by their feathery antennae and by their wings held flat against the back when at rest, fly quickly and mostly at night. Butterflies, with their more delicate bodies and fine, nobbed antennae, glide more slowly. They travel during the day. Some butterflies and moths are extremely strong, fast fliers capable of migrating thousands of miles and even crossing the Atlantic. Others are so weak that even flying to the next flower is exhausting.

Most butterflies and moths live only a short time. Before dying, they mate and lay eggs on the host plants. Some species lay eggs in or just under the bark on fruit trees; others deposit them in developing fruits or on the underside of leaves. Usually, the winter is passed in the egg stage and, in the spring, a new generation of plant-eating larvae is born.

Caterpillars are eaten by so many animals and attacked by so many diseases, that it is amazing that any ever become pests in the garden. Birds, some reptiles, and many predatory insects eat them. Various wasps parasitize them. They are infested by many different bacteria and viruses.

When these natural enemies fail to keep caterpillar populations under control, the next step should be handpicking. Many species are quite visible. Remove them by hand and destroy them. Cut out the nests of tent caterpillars and webworms. Fruitworms can be controlled by destroying infested fruits and by cultivating thoroughly and frequently. Gardeners are advised to understand the winter quarters of these insects. Learn to recognize them in the egg, pupal, and larval stages so that you can check their populations before they get out of hand.

Caterpillars that feed on foliage will often leave their host plants if an onion or hot pepper spray is applied. Try various other aromatics in an attempt to make the caterpillar "think" the plant is something it doesn't like.

Since they are soft bodied and slow moving, caterpillars are very susceptible to contact insecticides and barriers. If all else fails, try sabadilla dust, false hellebore, or rotenone. Diatomaceous earth suspended in water can control many species. A simple dust of flour or lime that coats the larva and eventually suffocates it may also interrupt the insect's life cycle.

CATERPILLAR
Apple-and-thorn Skeletonizer
Anthophila pariana

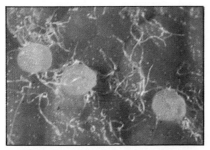

Oregon / Eggs

Oregon / Adult

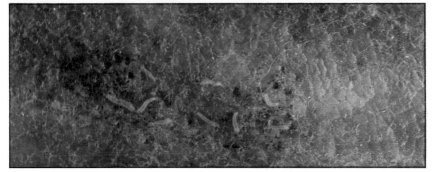

Oregon / Larvae

Range: Eastern United States and the Pacific Northwest.

Description: Yellowish green with a brown head and small, black protuberances on body; usually surrounded by a mass of webbing and frass; about ½ inch long. ADULT: Dark brown moth. EGGS: Laid on leaves and bark in the spring.

Life Cycle: Several generations per year. Overwinters as an adult moth in a protected spot.

Host Plants: Apple, quince.

Feeding Habits: Larvae web together the upper surfaces of leaves and twigs and feed on leaves and fruits within. Feeding does not usually cause significant damage to the host.

½″

CATERPILLAR
Army Cutworm
Euxoa auxiliaris

Jenkins / Larva

Range: Central and western United States.

Description: Brown or gray with distinct light and dark stripes; 1½ to 2 inches long. ADULT: Grayish brown moth with a kidney-shaped mark on each fore wing; 1½- to 2-inch wingspan. EGGS: White, round; laid in the soil.

Similar Insects: Beet armyworm (p. 98); fall armyworm (p. 107).

Life Cycle: One brood per year. Hibernates in the egg stage.

Host Plants: All garden vegetables.

Feeding Habits: Feeds just below the soil surface or just above it, severing the stems of seedlings.

Natural Controls: Wrap a paper collar around the stems of seedlings when they are set out. If the damage is intolerable, use *Bacillus thuringiensis*.

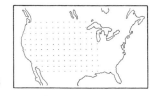

2″

CATERPILLAR
Artichoke Plume Moth
Platyptilia carduidactyla

Ross / Adult

Range: Throughout North America.

Description: Green or yellowish with black shields on the head, thorax, and anus; hairy; lives in webs; ½ inch long. ADULT: Brownish moth with featherlike wings; wings are closed and stretched out at right angles to the body when at rest; 1-inch wingspan. EGGS: Laid on branches and stems.

Life Cycle: Up to three generations per year. Hibernates in the larval stage.

Host Plants: Artichoke, similar species feed on grape.

Feeding Habits: Caterpillars chew new leaves and bore into stems, stalks, and buds, particularly in the spring.

Natural Controls: For grape, spray with dormant oil just as buds swell; for artichoke, bury old plant tops and destroy wormy plants.

½″

CATERPILLAR
Beet Armyworm/Asparagus Fern Caterpillar
Spodoptera exigua

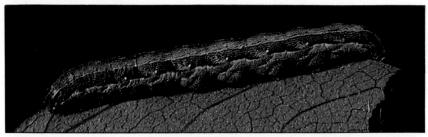

Badgley / Larva

Badgley / Adult

Range: Throughout North America.

Description: Green with yellow underside and dark green and yellow stripes; 1 to 2 inches long. ADULT: Mottled gray moth with two yellow spots near the centers of the fore wings; night flying; 1-inch wingspan. EGGS: Laid on bark in masses and covered with hair.

Similar Insects: Army cutworm (p. 96); fall armyworm (p. 107).

Life Cycle: Five to six generations per year. Adults migrate south in the winter.

Host Plants: Beet, corn, pea, pepper, spinach, tomato.

Feeding Habits: Caterpillars chew foliage and buds. They travel in large groups and may be very destructive.

Insect Predators: Trichogramma wasps.

Natural Controls: Handpicking is usually adequate, but apply *Bacillus thuringiensis* to serious infestations.

2″

CATERPILLAR
Cabbage Looper
Trichoplusia ni

Badgley / Larva

Badgley / Adult

Kriner / Eggs (cabbage looper, top; imported cabbageworm, bottom)

Range: United States and southern Canada.

Description: Green with pale stripes down the back; loops its body as it crawls; 1½ inches long. ADULT: Brownish with a silvery spot in the middle of each fore wing; night flying; 1½-inch wingspan. EGGS: Greenish white, round; laid singly on the upper surface of leaves.

Similar Insects: Diamondback moth (p. 104); garden webworm (p. 112); imported cabbageworm (p. 117).

Life Cycle: Several broods per year. Winter is spent as a pupa attached to a leaf, but in northern regions adults may migrate south for the winter.

Host Plants: Bean, broccoli, cabbage, cauliflower, celery, kale, lettuce, parsley, pea, potato, radish, spinach, tomato.

Feeding Habits: Larvae chew leaves.

Insect Predators: Trichogramma wasps.

Natural Controls: Use *Bacillus thuringiensis* for serious infestations.

1½"

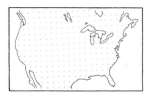

CATERPILLAR
Codling Moth
Carpocapsa pomonella

Roberts / Pupa

Kriner / Adult

Badgley / Larva

Range: Throughout North America.

Description: Pink with brown head; 1 inch long. ADULT: Grayish brown moth with lacy brown lines on the fore wings and pale, fringed hind wings; ¾-inch wingspan. EGGS: White; flat; laid singly on leaves, twigs, or fruit buds.

Similar Insects: Lesser peachtree borer (p. 64); navel orangeworm (p. 119); peachtree borer (p. 66).

Life Cycle: Two generations per year. Passes the winter in a cocoon beneath bark or in orchard litter.

Host Plants: Apple, pear, quince, walnut.

Feeding Habits: Larvae enter young apples at the blossom end, and when fully grown, tunnel out leaving brown excrement on the outside. Later in the season, second-brood larvae enter fruits from any end.

Insect Predators: A braconid wasp *(Ascogaster quadridentata),* some trichogramma wasps.

Natural Controls: In the spring, wrap trunk with corrugated paper. Spray trees with ryania or, during the egg stage, spray with a dormant-oil solution.

1″

Kriner / Eggs

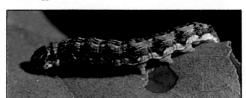

Badgley / Leaf-eating larva

Badgley / Pupa

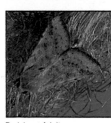

Badgley / Adult

Kriner / Larva

Range: Throughout North America.

Description: Color varies from white to green and even red with four pairs of prolegs; spined; 1½ inches long. ADULT: Greenish gray or brown moth with black markings on the fore wings; night flying; 1½-inch wingspan. EGGS: Light brown or yellow; domed, ridged; laid singly on plant leaves.

Similar Insects: European corn borer (p. 61).

Life Cycle: Up to seven generations per year. Pupa passes winter in soil.

Host Plants: Bean, corn, pea, pepper, potato, squash, tomato.

Feeding Habits: Earworms chew buds and leaves, causing plants to be stunted. Later, they enter corn ears at the tip and work their way to the kernels. Masses of moist castings result; pollination is hindered; mold forms. On tomato, larvae enter the stem end. Larvae chew foliage of other crops.

Insect Predators: Tachinid fly *(Lydella stabulans grisescens).*

Natural Controls: *Bacillus thuringiensis* for serious infestations on garden vegetables. On corn, apply a drop of mineral oil inside the tip of each ear after silk has wilted.

1½″

CATERPILLAR
Cotton Square Borer / Gray Hairstreak
Strymon melinus

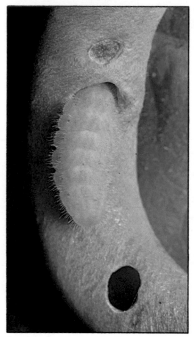

Ross / Larva   Ross / Adult

Range: Throughout North America.

Description: Bright green to yellowish; covered with fine hairs; ½ inch long. ADULT: Bluish or gray butterfly with black and orange spots on the wings; when at rest, it rubs together its two hind wings; 1-inch wingspan. EGGS: Green; laid singly on foliage.

Life Cycle: Several generations per year. Passes the winter in the egg stage.

Host Plants: Apple, bean (particularly lima), citrus.

Feeding Habits: Larvae chew leaves, later fruits and pods, but the damage is not very serious or extensive.

Insect Predators: Various trichogramma wasps.

Natural Controls: Apply *Bacillus thuringiensis* if damage is intolerable.

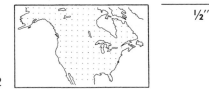

½"

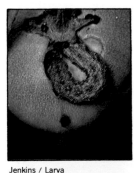

Jenkins / Larva

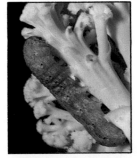

Ross / Larva

Jenkins / Larva

Moreton / Adult

Jenkins / Larva

Range: Various species throughout North America.

Description: Grayish or brown; curls up when disturbed; seldom seen during the day; 1 to 2 inches long. ADULT: Gray or brownish moth with paler hind wings; night flying, attracted to lights; 1- to 1½-inch wingspan. EGGS: Usually laid in the soil.

Life Cycle: One to five generations, depending upon species. Winter is passed as a pupa or young larva.

Host Plants: All garden vegetables, particularly seedlings and transplants.

Feeding Habits: Larvae feed near the soil surface, cutting stems several inches below ground level or just above it.

Insect Predators: Trichogramma wasps.

Natural Controls: Place a collar of stiff paper or cardboard around each plant when it is transplanted to the garden. *Bacillus thuringiensis* kills the larvae.

2″

CATERPILLAR
Diamondback Moth
Plutella xylostella

Oregon / Damage

Oregon / Adult

Range: Throughout North America.

Description: Pale green with a black head; tapered body; wriggles and hangs from a silken thread; 1/5 inch long. ADULT: Gray moth with folded yellow diamond-shaped areas on the wings; 3/4-inch wingspan. EGGS: Yellow; laid singly on foliage.

Similar Insects: Cabbage looper (p. 99); garden webworm (p. 112); imported cabbageworm (p. 117).

Life Cycle: Two to six generations per year. Moths hibernate in cabbage debris.

Host Plants: Broccoli, cabbage, cauliflower, kohlrabi.

Feeding Habits: Larvae mine leaves, then feed externally, seldom causing serious injury.

Natural Controls: *Bacillus thuringiensis* and other treatments for cabbage caterpillars will work.

1/5"

CATERPILLAR
Eastern Tent Caterpillar
Malacosoma americanum

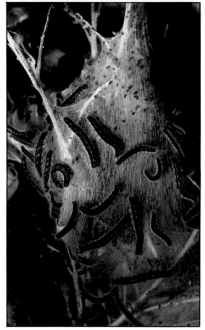

McKeever / Adult

Ross / Tent of western species

Range: Eastern and central United States. Similar species in the West.

Description: Black with white stripes and narrower brown and yellow lines on the sides and a row of blue spots; hairy; 2 inches long. ADULT: Reddish brown with stripes on the fore wings; 1- to 1½-inch wingspan. EGGS: Laid in a ring around twigs and covered with a shiny, hard substance.

Similar Insects: Forest tent caterpillar (p. 110).

Life Cycle: One generation per year. Winter is passed in the egg stage.

Host Plants: Apple, pear, and other fruit trees.

Feeding Habits: Larvae make webbed tents in the forks and crotches of trees and feed within.

Insect Predators: Various ground beetles and predaceous wasps.

Natural Controls: *Bacillus thuringiensis* controls the larvae.

2″

CATERPILLAR
Eyespotted Bud Moth
Spilonota ocellana

Oregon / Adult

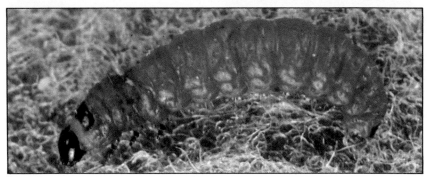

Kriner / Larva

Range: Northern United States and southern Canada. Similar species throughout North America.

Description: Brown with shiny black head and black shields on the head and anus; 1/3 inch long. ADULT: Gray moth with a white band across the fore wings; 1/2-inch wingspan. EGGS: Clear; saucer shaped; laid on the underside of leaves.

Life Cycle: One brood per year. Larvae hibernate in silky white cocoons attached to twigs.

Host Plants: Apple, cherry, pear, plum.

Feeding Habits: Larvae feed on blossoms in the spring and form webs where they chew the underside of leaves and make pits in developing fruits. Similar species mine leaves.

Natural Controls: *Bacillus thuringiensis* helps control the caterpillars.

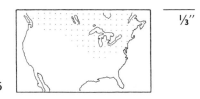

1/3"

CATERPILLAR
Fall Armyworm/Budworm
Spodoptera frugiperda

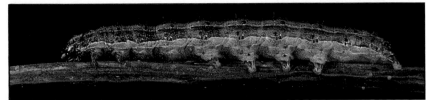

O.A.R.D.C. / Larva

Kriner / Larvae in corn

Range: Most of the United States, except the Far North. Similar species throughout North America.

Description: Brown with a black head, yellow stripes down the back; V-shaped white mark on the head; somewhat hairy; young white larvae hang from threads or curl up in leaves; 1¾ inches long. ADULT: Gray, mottled moth (females with pinkish or white wing margins); 1½-inch wingspan. EGGS: Covered with hair; laid in groups of 50 to 150 on host plants.

Similar Insects: Army cutworm (p. 96); beet armyworm (p. 98).

Life Cycle: One to six generations per year. Adults migrate south for the winter.

Host Plants: Bean, beet, cabbage, corn, cucumber, potato, spinach, sweet potato, tomato, turnip, and other vegetables.

Feeding Habits: Larvae feed on grasses and corn in early spring, later chewing stems near the ground. Feeding occurs at night.

Insect Predators: Trichogramma wasps.

Natural Controls: Apply *Bacillus thuringiensis* to kill larvae.

1¾"

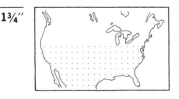

CATERPILLAR
Fall Cankerworm
Alsophila pometaria

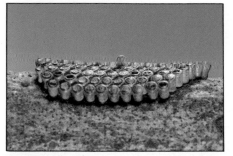
Visual Teaching / Eggs

Kriner / Wingless adult

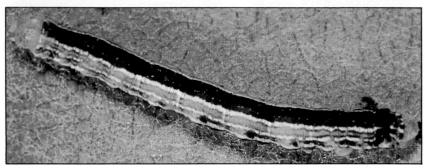
Kriner / Larva

Range: Southeastern Canada and northeastern and central United States.

Description: Brownish green with whitish stripes; ¾ inch long. ADULT: Brown or grayish moth with white wing bands; 1-inch wingspan. EGGS: Brown or grayish; shaped like flowerpots; laid in compact masses on trunk or branches.

Similar Insects: Spring cankerworm (p. 131).

Life Cycle: One generation per year. Overwinters in the egg stage.

Host Plants: Apple, cherry.

Feeding Habits: Larvae chew holes in leaves and spin silken threads.

Natural Controls: Band trunks with a sticky material such as Tanglefoot or spray with *Bacillus thuringiensis*.

¾″

CATERPILLAR
Fall Webworm
Hyphantria cunea

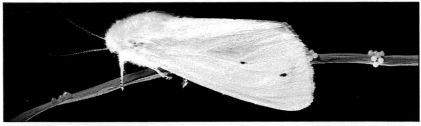

Heilman / Adult

Ross / Larva

Range: United States and southern Canada.

Description: Pale green or yellow; covered with long, silky hairs attached to small humps; 1 inch long. ADULT: White with brown spots; 2-inch wingspan. EGGS: Laid in masses on the underside of leaves and covered with hairs.

Similar Insects: Eastern tent caterpillar (p. 105); saltmarsh caterpillar (p. 130); yellow woollybear (p. 138).

Life Cycle: One to three or four generations per year. Pupae overwinter in cocoons attached to tree bark or orchard trash.

Host Plants: Apple, cherry, peach, pecan, walnut.

Feeding Habits: Caterpillars make silken nests on the ends of branches and feed on leaves.

Insect Predators: Various trichogramma wasps.

Natural Controls: Apply *Bacillus thuringiensis* if the damage is intolerable.

1″

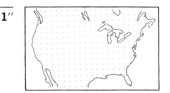

CATERPILLAR
Forest Tent Caterpillar
Malacosoma disstria

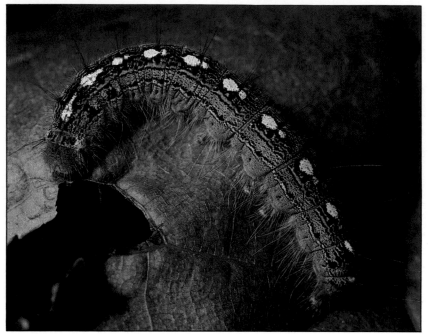

Carr / Larva

Range: Throughout North America.

Description: Pale blue to black with diamond-shaped white marks down the middle of the back and a blue head; 2 inches long. ADULT: Light yellow to brown with darker markings; 1-inch wingspan. EGGS: Laid in bands around twigs.

Similar Insects: Eastern tent caterpillar (p. 105).

Life Cycle: One brood per year. Winter is passed in the egg stage.

Host Plants: Apple, cherry, peach, pear, plum, quince.

Feeding Habits: Larvae chew leaves and spin cocoons, but do not form tents.

Natural Controls: *Bacillus thuringiensis* can be used if the damage is intolerable.

2"

CATERPILLAR
Fruittree Leafroller
Archips argyrospilus

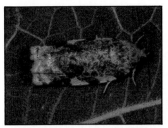

Jenkins / Adult

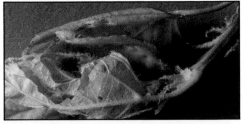

Oregon / Damage

Jenkins / Larva

Range: Throughout North America.

Description: Green with dark brown head; covered with fine spines; 1 inch long. ADULT: Brownish yellow moth with mottling and two beige spots on the wing margins; ¾-inch wingspan. EGGS: Pale yellow to brown, covered with a brownish varnish; laid in masses of up to 100 on twigs and branches.

Life Cycle: One generation per year. Hibernates as an egg.

Host Plants: Apple and other fruit trees.

Feeding Habits: Larvae spin webs around leaves at the tops of branches and feed on bugs, leaves, and small fruits. Mature apples have deep, russeted scars.

Insect Predators: Various trichogramma wasps.

Natural Controls: Dormant-oil spray applied just before buds open or *Bacillus thuringiensis* after the caterpillars appear.

1″

CATERPILLAR
Garden Webworm
Achyra rantalis

Badgley / Adult

Jenkins / Larvae

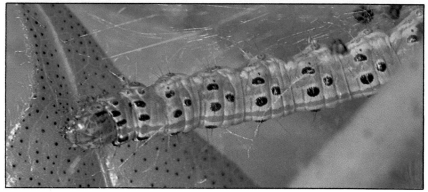

Badgley / Larva

Range: Throughout North America.

Description: Green with a light stripe; several hairs on each segment; ¾ inch long. ADULT: Brownish yellow moth with gray and brown markings; ¾-inch wingspan. EGGS: Laid in clusters on the leaves.

Life Cycle: Two to four generations. Pupae overwinter in the soil.

Host Plants: Bean, beet, corn, pea, strawberry.

Feeding Habits: Larvae spin light webs and feed within, dropping to the ground when disturbed.

Insect Predators: Various trichogramma wasps.

Natural Controls: Use *Bacillus thuringiensis* or pyrethrum for intolerable infestations.

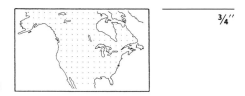

¾"

CATERPILLAR
Grape Berry Moth
Endopiza viteana

Jenkins / Larva

Range: Northeastern United States and southeastern Canada.

Description: Green with a brown head; ½ inch long. ADULT: Gray to purple moth; ½-inch wingspan. EGGS: Cream colored; flat, disc shaped; laid on stems, flowers, or berries.

Life Cycle: One to three generations per year. Winter is spent in a cocoon enclosed in a fallen leaf.

Host Plants: Grape.

Feeding Habits: Larvae web together berries and leaves as they feed. Infested grapes ripen prematurely and fall before fully grown. A small hole can be seen in some.

Insect Predators: Ground beetles, several wasps.

Natural Controls: Remove litter and fallen leaves after grapes have been harvested and cultivate in early spring. If necessary, use *Bacillus thuringiensis*.

½″

CATERPILLAR
Grapeleaf Skeletonizer
Harrisina sp.

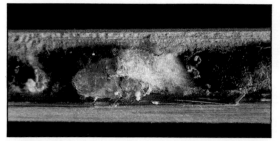

Badgley / Cocoons

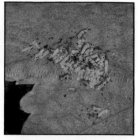

Badgley / First instar

Badgley / Third and fifth instars

Badgley / Adult

Range: United States.

Description: Yellow with black bands just behind the head; eastern species with an orange collar; long black hairs on each segment; 1 inch long. ADULT: Dark gray or metallic blue moth; narrow wings; 1-inch wingspan. EGGS: Laid in clusters on leaves.

Life Cycle: Three generations per year. Pupae overwinter in cocoons in bark or ground litter.

Host Plants: Grape.

Feeding Habits: Larvae feed between the veins on the underside of leaves. They form neat, compact colonies. Controls are seldom needed.

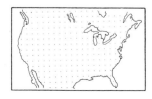

1″

CATERPILLAR
Green Fruitworm
Lithophane antennata

O.A.R.D.C. / Larva

Range: Northern United States and southern Canada.

Description: Light green, with a stripe on the sides and brown head; thick bodied, short; 1 inch long. ADULT: Gray or purple moth with darker mottling; 1½-inch wingspan. EGGS: Laid singly on branches in early spring.

Similar Insects: Pyramidal fruitworm (p. 127).

Life Cycle: One generation per year. Adults hibernate in sheltered areas near the orchard.

Host Plants: Apple, cherry, peach, pear, plum, quince.

Feeding Habits: Larvae chew leaves and bore into green fruits, causing shallow cavities to form. Fruits may drop, but usually injury is minimal. Injured fruits heal over quickly.

Natural Controls: Apply *Bacillus thuringiensis* when damage is intolerable.

1"

CATERPILLAR
Gypsy Moth
Lymantria dispar

Henley / Hatching larvae

Visual Teaching / Adult (male)

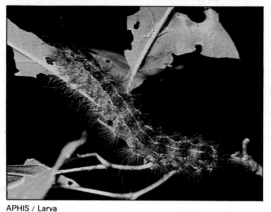

APHIS / Larva

Visual Teaching / Adult (female)

Range: Eastern United States.

Description: Gray with long brown hair; flat; nocturnal; 2 inches long. ADULT: Gray (male) or white (female) moth with a hairy body; 1½- to 2-inch wingspan. EGGS: Light brown to yellowish; laid in groups of 400 and covered with hair.

Similar Insects: Western tussock moth (p. 135).

Life Cycle: One generation per year. Winter is passed in the egg stage.

Host Plants: Apple, cherry.

Feeding Habits: Masses of caterpillars feed on foliage at night, hiding in orchard litter during the day.

Insect Predators: Trichogramma wasps eat the eggs.

Natural Controls: Apply *Bacillus thuringiensis* to the caterpillars.

2″

CATERPILLAR
Imported Cabbageworm
Pieris rapae

Ross / Adult

Badgley / Damage

Jenkins / Larva and pupa

Range: Throughout North America.

Description: Velvety pale green with yellow stripe; leaves behind dark green pellets of excrement; 1¼ inches long. ADULT: White moth with black tip on the fore wing and two or three black spots; 1- to 2-inch wingspan. EGGS: Yellowish; bullet shaped; ridged; laid singly on the leaves. (See photograph on p. 99.)

Similar Insects: Cabbage looper (p. 99); diamondback moth (p. 104); garden webworm (p. 112).

Life Cycle: Two to three generations per year. Hibernation is in the pupal stage.

Host Plants: Cabbage, cauliflower, kale, kohlrabi, mustard, radish, turnip.

Feeding Habits: Caterpillars feed on leaves, chewing huge holes in them.

Insect Predators: Various trichogramma wasps.

Natural Controls: *Bacillus thuringiensis* can be used on a large scale, but first try dusting with a flour-and-salt mixture or spraying leaves with sour milk or a garlic infusion.

1¼"

117

CATERPILLAR
Io Moth
Automeris io

Gossington / Larva

Gossington / Adult

Range: Eastern and central North America.

Description: Green with a broad pink stripe and a thinner white one; many stiff, stinging hairs; 3 inches long. ADULT: Bright yellow or purplish moth with black eyespot on each hind wing; large, feathery antennae; hairy body; 2½- to 3-inch wingspan. EGGS: Laid on leaves and branches of host plants.

Life Cycle: One generation per year. Winter is passed in a cocoon on the ground.

Host Plants: Apple, blackberry, corn, currant.

Feeding Habits: Larvae chew foliage but seldom cause serious damage. Spines are very irritating so do not touch these insects.

3″

Badgley / Adult

Badgley / Larva

Badgley / Pupa

Range: Southwestern and western United States.

Description: Reddish orange to yellowish with brown head and two parenthesis-shaped marks just behind the head; ¾ inch long. ADULT: Gray moth with dark diagonal stripes and mottling; ¾-inch wingspan. EGGS: Laid in the blossom end of fruits and nuts.

Similar Insects: Codling moth (p. 100).

Life Cycle: One generation per year. Larvae overwinter in dropped fruits or nuts.

Host Plants: Almond, citrus, fig, walnut.

Feeding Habits: Caterpillars drill holes in diseased or damaged fruits and nuts. They feed within webs, then pupate and exit as fully grown moths.

Natural Controls: Harvest crops early and eliminate orchard trash.

¾″

CATERPILLAR
Obliquebanded Leafroller/Rose Leaftier
Choristoneura rosaceana

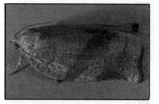
Oregon / Adult

Oregon / Larva

Henley / Web

Range: Throughout North America.

Description: Pale green with a black head; ½ to 1 inch long. ADULT: Grayish brown moth; ¾-inch wingspan. EGGS: Green; laid in overlapping masses on the underside of leaves.

Life Cycle: One brood per year. Hibernates in a cocoon.

Host Plants: Apple, apricot, bean, blackberry, celery, cherry, currant, peach, pear, raspberry, strawberry.

Feeding Habits: Larvae mine leaves in early spring, later forming webs and rolling together leaves as they feed.

Natural Controls: Remove and destroy infested leaves and branches. On a large scale, spray with a mixture of pyrethrum and rotenone or with *Bacillus thuringiensis.*

1″

CATERPILLAR
Omnivorous Leaftier/Strawberry Fruitworm
Cnephasia longana

Oregon / Larva and damage

Oregon / Adult

Range: California and the Pacific Northwest.

Description: Cream colored with white stripes along the sides; ¼ inch long. ADULT: Tan moth with darker spots on the fore wings; ½-inch wingspan. EGGS: Laid on bark or rough wood.

Life Cycle: One generation per year. Larvae pass the winter in bark crevices.

Host Plants: Bean, pea, strawberry.

Feeding Habits: Larvae make webs and feed on foliage and fruits.

Natural Controls: Handpick the larvae and clean up garden litter. Apply *Bacillus thuringiensis* if necessary.

¼"

CATERPILLAR
Orangedog/Giant Swallowtail
Papilio cresphontes

Gossington / Adult

Gossington / Larva

Roberts / Larvae

Range: Southeastern Canada and eastern and southern United States; similar species in the Southwest.

Description: Dark brown with beige or yellowish markings; one end resembles the nose of a dog with two black spots as eyes; 2½ inches long. ADULT: Dark green butterfly with yellow bands across the wings; 5½-inch wingspan. EGGS: Whitish pink; laid in new shoots in early spring.

Similar Insects: Parsleyworm (p. 125).

Life Cycle: One to three generations per year. In cold regions, larvae spend the winter in pupal chambers.

Host Plants: Citrus.

Feeding Habits: Larvae chew foliage and may even defoliate young trees if they are not removed by hand.

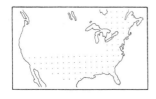

2½"

CATERPILLAR
Orange Tortrix
Argyrotaenia citrana

Oregon / Larva

Oregon / Adult

Oregon / Pupa

Range: Southwestern United States and the Far West.

Description: Pale green or gold with light brown head; ½ inch long. ADULT: Tan- to rust-colored moth with black bands forming a V when wings are folded at rest; ½-inch wingspan. EGGS: Yellowish; laid in overlapping masses.

Life Cycle: Two to four generations per year. Larvae overwinter in garden litter.

Host Plants: Apple, apricot, citrus, pear, plum.

Feeding Habits: Larvae make nests and pupate in leaves and flowers at the tips of twigs. They feed on foliage.

Natural Controls: Destroy eggs as they appear and catch adult moths with light traps. *Bacillus thuringiensis* kills the larvae.

½"

CATERPILLAR
Oriental Fruit Moth
Grapholitha molesta

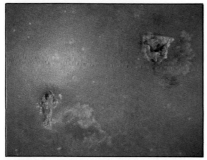

Roberts / Damage

Jenkins / Larva in peach

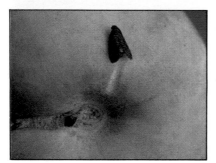

Jenkins / Adult

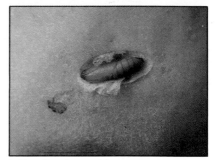

Jenkins / Pupa

Range: Eastern North America and the Pacific Northwest.

Description: Grayish white to pink with brown head and brown markings on the thorax; usually in a white web; ½ inch long. ADULT: Gray moth with brown markings; ½-inch wingspan. EGGS: White; flat; laid on the underside of leaves or on twigs.

Similar Insects: Codling moth (p. 100); lesser peachtree borer (p. 64); navel orangeworm (p. 119); peachtree borer (p. 66).

Life Cycle: Four to seven generations per year. Hibernates in its cocoon in tree bark or on the ground.

Host Plants: Almond, apple, apricot, cherry, peach, pear, plum.

Feeding Habits: Larvae bore into young twigs and later enter fruits at the stem end. There is no external damage to fruits, only tunnelling within.

Insect Predators: A braconid wasp *(Macrocentrus ancylivorus)*, a trichogramma wasp *(Trichogramma minutum).*

Natural Controls: Cultivate the soil 4 inches deep, several weeks before trees bloom. Use *Bacillus thuringiensis* to kill larvae.

½″

CATERPILLAR
Parsleyworm / Celeryworm / Black Swallowtail Butterfly
Papilio polyxenes asterius

McKeever / Adult   Ross / Larva

McKeever / Chrysalis

Range: Throughout North America.

Description: Brown with white on the middle of the back; later, green with white-spotted black band on each segment and two orange horns that project when the insect is disturbed; 2 inches long. ADULT: Black butterfly with yellow spots on the edges of the wings; taillike projection on the hind wings; 3-inch wingspan. EGGS: White; laid singly on leaves of host plants.

Similar Insects: Orangedog (p. 122).

Life Cycle: Two to four generations per year. Passes the winter as a pupa or, in the South, as an adult.

Host Plants: Carrot, celery, parsley, parsnip.

Feeding Habits: Larvae chew leaves and stems but, since few are present, they do little damage.

Natural Controls: Apply *Bacillus thuringiensis* if handpicking is not adequate.

2″

CATERPILLAR
Puss Caterpillar
Megalopyge opercularis

Gossington / Cocoon

Gossington / Larva

Gossington / Adult

Range: Southeastern United States.

Description: Green to brown with long white to reddish hair covering stinging spines; flat and broad; ¾ to 1 inch long. ADULT: Beige moth with dark markings; 1-inch wingspan. EGGS: Laid on foliage or bark.

Similar Insects: Fall webworm (p. 109); saltmarsh caterpillar (p. 130); yellow woollybear (p. 138).

Life Cycle: One generation per year. Winter is passed in cocoons attached to tree branches.

Host Plants: Usually found on certain ornamentals, but may occur on orchard trees.

Feeding Habits: Larvae feed alone on foliage, doing no harm. Do not touch these caterpillars since their spines are very poisonous.

1″

CATERPILLAR
Pyramidal Fruitworm
Amphipyra pyramidoides

O.A.R.D.C. / Larva

Range: Throughout most of North America.

Description: Bright green with a hump near the head; ¾ inch long. ADULT: Brown or grayish moth with orange hind wings. EGGS: Laid on bark and branches of trees.

Similar Insects: Green fruitworm (p. 115).

Life Cycle: One generation per year. Hibernates in the egg stage.

Host Plants: Most fruit trees.

Feeding Habits: Larvae feed on young foliage and green fruits in early summer.

Natural Controls: Late-summer cultivation is the best control.

¾″

127

CATERPILLAR
Redbanded Leafroller
Argyrotaenia velutinana

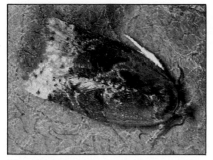

Kriner / Adult

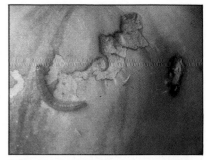

Jenkins / Larva and damage

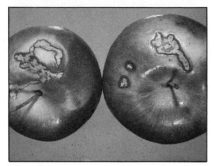

Kriner / Damage

Kriner / Eggs

Range: Eastern North America.

Description: Pale green with yellowish marks on the thorax and head; slender; ¾ inch long. ADULT: White moth with reddish band on fore wings; ½-inch wingspan. EGGS: Yellow; laid in overlapping masses on bark, foliage, or fruits.

Life Cycle: Two or three generations per year. Hibernates as a pupa in garden litter.

Host Plants: Most vegetables and fruits, particularly apple.

Feeding Habits: Larvae feed on leaves early in season and spin fine webs. Later, they chew patches in the surface of fruits.

Insect Predators: Trichogramma and other wasps.

Natural Controls: Apply *Bacillus thuringiensis* to serious infestations.

¾″

CATERPILLAR
Redhumped Caterpillar / Redhumped Appleworm
Schizura concinna

Ross / Larva

Range: Throughout North America.

Description: Yellow with red and white stripes, a red head, and a bright red hump; black spines on several segments; 1½ inches long. ADULT: Grayish brown moth; males with dark markings; 1½-inch wingspan.

Similar Insects: Yellownecked caterpillar (p. 137).

Life Cycle: One generation per year. Winter is spent in a cocoon in the soil.

Host Plants: Apple, apricot, blackberry, cherry, pear, plum, sweet gum, walnut.

Feeding Habits: Larvae feed in colonies, clinging to leaves and branches as they skeletonize leaves. Infested trees may be defoliated.

Natural Controls: Remove colonies by pruning and burn them. Apply *Bacillus thuringiensis* to serious infestations.

1½″

CATERPILLAR
Saltmarsh Caterpillar
Estigmene acrea

Ross / Adult

Ross / Larva

Range: Throughout North America.

Description: Gray to reddish brown with a black head; hairy; 2 inches long. ADULT: Orangish yellow and white moth with black spots or nearly all white; 2- to 2½-inch wingspan. EGGS: Laid by the thousands on the underside of leaves.

Similar Insects: Fall webworm (p. 109); yellow woollybear (p. 138).

Life Cycle: One generation per year. Hibernates as a mature larva.

Host Plants: Apple, asparagus, bean, beet, cabbage, carrot, celery, corn, lettuce, onion, plum.

Feeding Habits: Larvae feed in masses on the underside of leaves, often defoliating an entire tree or ruining whole fields of crops.

Insect Predators: Tachinid flies *(Exorista mella* and *Leschenaultia adusta).*

Natural Controls: If the problem is intolerable, apply *Bacillus thuringiensis.*

2″

CATERPILLAR
Spring Cankerworm
Paleacrita vernata

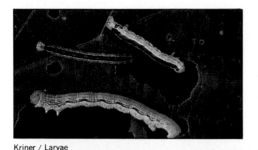
Kriner / Larvae

Oregon / Adult

Kriner / Larvae and damage

Range: Most of the United States and southern Canada.

Description: Light green to dark brown with whitish lines down the back; three pairs of prolegs; ¾ inch long. ADULT: Light brown or gray moth with translucent wings; 1-inch wingspan. EGGS: Brownish purple; laid in groups beneath the bark.

Similar Insects: Fall cankerworm (p. 108).

Life Cycle: One brood per year. Hibernates in the soil.

Host Plants: Apple.

Feeding Habits: Larvae feed on foliage, often dropping down on silk threads then climbing back to resume feeding. They tend to appear in cycles of two or three years.

Insect Predators: Trichogramma wasps.

Natural Controls: Trap cankerworms by banding trees with a sticky material such as Tanglefoot during egg-laying time.

¾″

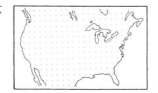

CATERPILLAR
Strawberry Crown Moth
Synanthedon bibionipennis

Oregon / Larva   Oregon / Adult

Range: Throughout North America.

Description: White to yellow or pinkish caterpillar with brown head; ½ inch long. ADULT: Black and yellow, clear-winged moth; 1–inch wingspan. EGGS: Laid on underside of lower leaves in midsummer.

Similar Insects: Raspberry crown borer (p. 70); yellow jacket (p. 23).

Life Cycle: One generation per year. Larvae pass the winter in strawberry crowns.

Host Plants: Blackberry, raspberry, strawberry.

Feeding Habits: Groups of larvae bore into crowns causing foliage to yellow. Recent transplants may die; older plants are weakened.

Natural Controls: Pull and burn infested plants in early spring.

½″

CATERPILLAR
Tomato Hornworm
Manduca quinquemaculata

Badgley / Egg   Jenkins / Pupae   Badgley / Adult

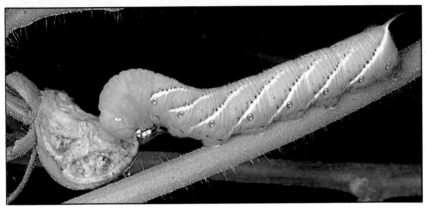

Moreton / Larva (tobacco hornworm)

Range: Throughout North America.

Description: Green with seven or eight white stripes and a black horn project-ing from the rear; similar species, tobacco hornworm *(M. sexta)*, shown in above photograph, has a red horn; 3 to 4 inches long. ADULT: Grayish or brownish moth with white zigzags on the rear wings and orange or brownish spots on the body; 4- to 5-inch wingspan. EGGS: Greenish yellow; laid on the underside of leaves.

Life Cycle: One to two generations per year. Winter is passed in the pupal stage.

Host Plants: Eggplant, pepper, potato, tomato.

Feeding Habits: Larvae chew leaves and fruits.

Insect Predators: Braconid wasps lay eggs on caterpillars, often forming small white cocoons on the skin. Trichogramma wasps parasitize hornworms in the egg stage.

Natural Controls: Plants can tolerate some feeding but if the caterpillars be-come a problem, remove them by hand.

4″

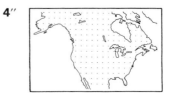

CATERPILLAR
Walnut Caterpillar
Datana integerrima

Jenkins / Larva

Range: Eastern and southern United States.

Description: Reddish brown to black with a black head; hairy; 2 inches long. ADULT: Brown moth with four dark bands bordered in white; hairy body; 1- to 2-inch wingspan. EGGS: Laid in masses on the underside of leaves.

Life Cycle: One to two generations per year. Pupae hibernate in the soil.

Host Plants: Apple, peach, pecan, walnut.

Feeding Habits: Larvae feed in groups, stopping to molt in midsummer, not resuming until fall.

Natural Controls: Destroy eggs and larvae as they appear. *Bacillus thuringiensis* or a pyrethrum spray may control the larvae.

2″

CATERPILLAR
Western Tussock Moth
Orgyia vetusta

Ross / Larva

Range: Western North America with a similar species in the East.

Description: Brown with yellow and black stripes and a bright red head; hairy; 1¼ inches long. ADULT: Gray moth with dark wavy bands (male) or wingless (female); 1¼-inch wingspan. EGGS: Laid in masses on the female's cocoon and covered with hairs.

Similar Insects: Gypsy moth (p. 116).

Life Cycle: One to three generations per year. Winter is passed in the egg stage.

Host Plants: Apple, apricot, peach, pear, plum, quince.

Feeding Habits: Larvae skeletonize leaves and form silken cocoons on bark.

Insect Predators: Various trichogramma wasps.

Natural Controls: Apply *Bacillus thuringiensis* to larvae and eggs.

1¼"

CATERPILLAR
Whitelined Sphinx Moth
Hyles lineata

 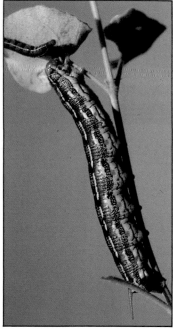

Badgley / Adult   Ross / Larva

Range: United States and southern Canada.

Description: Greenish yellow with a yellow horn and head and pale spots outlined in black; 2½ to 3 inches long. ADULT: Brown moth with white stripes running diagonally across the wings and a broad, buff-colored band; thick antennae; resembles a small hummingbird; 3-inch wingspan. EGGS: Laid on the underside of leaves.

Life Cycle: Two generations per year. Winter is passed in the pupal stage.

Host Plants: Beet, currant, grape, melon, pear, plum, tomato.

Feeding Habits: Hornworms feed on leaves and fruits, but they are easily controlled by handpicking.

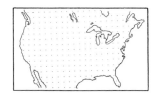

3″

CATERPILLAR
Yellownecked Caterpillar
Datana ministra

Gossington / Eggs

Schuder / Adult

Ross / Larva

Range: Throughout North America.

Description: Yellow and black striped with a yellow segment behind the head; covered with long white hairs; 1½ inches long. ADULT: Light brown with four dark, thin lines on the fore wings; 1- to 2-inch wingspan.

Similar Insects: Redhumped caterpillar (p. 129).

Life Cycle: One generation per year. Hibernates as a pupa in the soil.

Host Plants: Apple, apricot, blackberry, blueberry, cherry, peach, pecan, pear, plum, quince.

Feeding Habits: Caterpillars feed in compact colonies. They destroy leaf tissue and may defoliate entire branches.

Natural Controls: Shake larvae from the trees and destroy them. Dust with diatomaceous earth or apply *Bacillus thuringiensis*.

1½″

CATERPILLAR
Yellow Woollybear
Diacrisia virginica

Lemmo / Larva   Visual Teaching / Adult

Range: Throughout North America.

Description: Yellow, reddish, or white; covered with long hair; 1 to 1½ inches long. ADULT: White with a tiny black dot on each wing; 1½-inch wingspan. EGGS: Laid in large clusters on leaves and covered with hair.

Similar Insects: Fall webworm (p. 109); puss caterpillar (p. 126); saltmarsh caterpillar (p. 130).

Life Cycle: Several generations per year. Hibernates as a pupa in a silken cocoon.

Host Plants: Asparagus, bean, beet, cabbage, carrot, cauliflower, celery, cherry, corn, eggplant, grape, melon, pea, squash.

Feeding Habits: Caterpillars chew foliage and flower and fruit buds.

Insect Predators: Trichogramma wasps.

Natural Controls: *Bacillus thuringiensis* can be used for serious infestations.

1½"

CATERPILLAR
Zebra Caterpillar
Ceramica picta

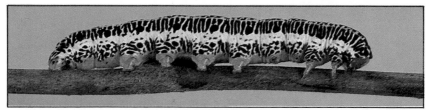

O.A.R.D.C. / Larva

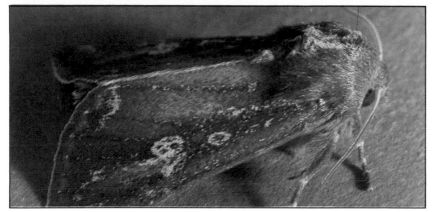

Oregon / Adult

Range: Throughout North America.

Description: Black with yellow stripes on both sides and many thin yellow lines; covered with fine, silky hair. ADULT: Rust or brownish moth.

Life Cycle: One generation per year. Winter is passed as a pupa.

Host Plants: Many garden vegetables and orchard crops.

Feeding Habits: Larvae chew foliage but rarely do serious damage. Controls are unnecessary.

CICADAS

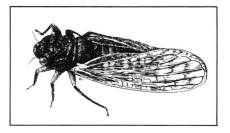

HOMOPTERA

Ranging from 1 to 2 inches in length, cicadas are the largest members of the order Homoptera. They have a wide, blunt head with prominent eyes and short, bristly antennae. Their clear, brittle wings are held over the body in a typical rooflike position. Their most conspicuous characteristic is an ability to produce sound. By vibrating a set of muscles against a pair of "drums" on the thorax, male cicadas create a loud, repetitious song.

Most cicadas spend only about five to six weeks above the ground as winged adults. For most of their lives, they grope about in the dark root systems of trees and sod. As nymphs, they have stout, brown bodies with large front legs that serve as scoops. They feed on roots and scrabble about blindly, passing through several moltings until they are ready to molt for the last time. Then, they dig their way out of the ground, climb a tree, and fasten their claws into the bark. Adults emerge through a split in the top of their nymphal skin. They feed for several weeks, mate, then lay eggs in slits made in tree twigs. Two months later, eggs hatch and a new generation of nymphs burrows into the soil.

There are two common types of cicadas: the *dogday* or *"harvestman"* cicadas that have two- to four-year life cycles, and the *periodical* cicadas that require 13 or even 17 years to complete their life cycles. Dogday cicadas are generally larger than periodical cicadas and appear in mid to late summer, rather than early summer. They seldom damage trees, but periodical species may injure fruit trees during egg laying.

To avoid problems with these insects, keep track of the years when large broods of cicadas are expected to emerge. Do not set out transplants until after eggs have been laid. Protect young fruit trees with mosquito netting. When broods are hatching, band trees with a sticky material, such as Tanglefoot or Stikem, that will trap the nymphs as they ascend the trunks. Prune injured twigs as soon as possible.

CICADA
Periodical Cicada
Magicicada septendecim

Roberts / Egg-laying damage

Ross / Adult

Roberts / Nymphs

Range: Thirteen-year race found in the eastern United States; 17-year race found mainly in the Southeast.

Description: Brown to blackish with orange legs and transparent wings; wedge shaped; 1 to 1½ inches long. EGGS: Inserted in slits made in the bark of twigs. NYMPH: Small, resembling brown ants when young. Later, brown to black; stout bodied.

Life Cycle: Thirteen or 17 years required to complete the life cycle. Nymphs remain underground until adulthood.

Host Plants: Apple.

Feeding Habits: Nymphs chew tree roots and adults suck sap from limbs and twigs, but neither do any damage. Injury comes from egg-laying slits that may cause tips of twigs to die.

Natural Controls: Remove injured twigs as soon as possible.

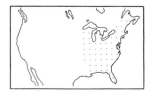

1½"

CRICKETS, GRASSHOPPERS, MANTIDS, AND WALKINGSTICKS

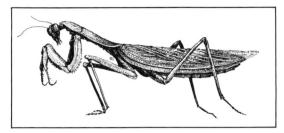

ORTHOPTERA

The order Orthoptera consists of insects with stiff fore wings which are not used in flying. These are generally long, narrow wings somewhat thickened and possessing many veins. When at rest, they are held over the abdomen in a rooflike position or they are held flat, overlapping each other. Membranous hind wings are folded beneath.

Many species rarely fly and some are entirely lacking in flight wings. Instead, they may rely on jumping and have enlarged legs that enable them to leap high and far. Grasshoppers and crickets use these hind legs to help thrust them into flight.

Grasshoppers and crickets are also distinguished by their ability to "sing." Although some females make soft noises, the males do most of the singing. Their music is usually a love call designed to attract a mate. Once they have found one, some species sing a courtship song. Others have fight songs and alarms as well.

These songs are made by rubbing together certain body parts. The loudest songsters, crickets, katydids, and longhorned grasshoppers, produce sound by stroking a ridged "file" on one fore wing with a sharp "scraper" on the other. Each stroke produces a gentle series of notes that are amplified through the wing surfaces. Other grasshoppers may rub together the fore wing and hind wing or use the upper leg to scrape the rough, outer edge of the fore wing.

Up to 200 strokes may occur per second, depending upon species and environment. Temperature is the major factor in cricket chirping. By counting the number of chirps per minute, subtracting 40, dividing by 4 and adding 50, you get the temperature in Fahrenheit degrees.

Metamorphosis is incomplete with nymphs usually passing through three to five molts before achieving adult size. During immature stages they closely resemble their adult counterparts but their wings are undersized. Eggs are laid on grass, weeds, or in the soil.

All members of the order chew their food. Mantids, a few species of grasshoppers, and some crickets are predaceous, but most orthopterans are planteaters. Shorthorned grasshoppers, characterized by their short antennae, have been destroying crops since biblical times. They feed on roots and leaves of many grains and sometimes damage garden crops or anything else that is available. Faced with starvation, they will grow longer flight wings and hind legs, thus equipping themselves for migration and for the desperate search for food.

Crickets may feed on plants, but they are rarely serious threats to crops. Mole crickets are sometimes a problem in nurseries where they chew plant roots. Snowy tree crickets may injure fruit trees during egg laying.

A number of natural enemies help control grasshoppers and crickets in the home garden. Crows, catbirds, bluebirds, mockingbirds, sparrows, and meadowlarks are among the many birds that feed on them. Spiders also eat them.

Netting or cheesecloth can be used to protect seedlings and fruit trees during migrations. Keep the garden well weeded and free of plant debris. Work the soil to expose eggs to predators and weather.

CRICKET
Field Cricket
Gryllus sp.

Ross / Adult

Range: Throughout North America.

Description: Dark brown or black; long antennae; wings folded flat along the sides; ¾ to 1 inch long. EGGS: Laid in damp soil.

Life Cycle: One to three generations per year. In the South, winter is passed in the nymph or adult stage; elsewhere in the egg stage.

Host Plants: Bean, cucumber, melon, squash, tomato.

Feeding Habits: Adults and nymphs chew foliage and flowers of young vegetable crops, but controls are rarely necessary.

1″

CRICKET
Jerusalem Cricket
Stenopelmatus fuscus

Ross / Jerusalem cricket adult

Lemmo / Camel cricket adult

Range: Western United States, particularly along the Pacific Coast. Many closely related species, such as the camel cricket found elsewhere.

Description: Brown with dark stripes across the abdomen; shiny; wingless; large head; spined legs; slow moving; 1½ inches long. EGGS: White, oval; laid in holes in the soil.

Life Cycle: One generation per year. Overwinters in the egg stage.

Host Plants: Potato; decaying plant material.

Feeding Habits: Adults and nymphs occasionally feed on potato tubers. Many eat other insects and are primarily beneficial.

1½″

CRICKET
Northern Mole Cricket
Neocurtilla hexadactyla

Jenkins / Adult

Range: Throughout North America.

Description: Brown with pale underside; hairy; strong nocturnal flier; front legs enlarged for burrowing; 1 to 1½ inches long. EGGS: Laid in the soil.

Life Cycle: One generation per year. All forms pass the winter in burrows in the soil.

Host Plants: Many garden and nursery plants.

Feeding Habits: Tunnelling in the upper inches of soil damages the roots of seedlings. Crickets also chew pits in the roots, eat seeds, and sever stems.

Natural Controls: Spray foliage and stems with a mixture of hot pepper, soap, and water.

1½″

CRICKET
Snowy Tree Cricket
Oecanthus fultoni

Jenkins / Adult

Range: Throughout North America.

Description: Whitish to pale green; slender; chirps at night; ½ inch long. EGGS: Deposited in lines of holes made in bark.

Life Cycle: One generation per year. Winter is passed in the egg stage.

Host Plants: Apple, blackberry, cherry, peach, plum.

Feeding Habits: Feeding is minimal and does not seriously injure plants. As nymphs, tree crickets may feed on small insects.

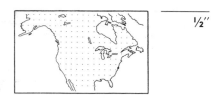

½″

GRASSHOPPER
Grasshoppers/Locusts
Acrididae

Ross / Adult

Range: Various species throughout North America.

Description: Brown to reddish yellow or green; long bodies with prominent jaws and short antennae; enlarged hind legs for jumping; 1 to 2 inches long. EGGS: Laid in egg pods in soil and weeds.

Life Cycle: One generation per year. Overwinters in the egg stage.

Host Plants: Most vegetable crops.

Feeding Habits: Grasshoppers feed during the day on leaves and stems, often defoliating plants during dry periods.

Natural Controls: Trap grasshoppers in mason jars partly filled with molasses and water and buried in the garden. Sprays of hot pepper, soap, and water may repel the insects.

2″

KATYDID
Broadwinged Katydid
Microcentrum rhombifolium

Ross / Adult

Range: Most of the United States, except the North.

Description: Green with large angular wings; 1½ inches long. EGGS: Grayish brown; flat; laid in double rows on twigs.

Life Cycle: One generation per year. Winter is passed in the egg stage.

Host Plants: Many orchard trees.

Feeding Habits: Katydids feed on foliage but since there are few of them, they do no significant damage.

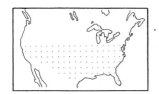

1½″

MANTID
Praying Mantids
Mantidae

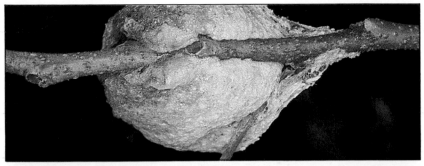

Moreton / Egg mass

Rodale / Adult

Range: Various species throughout North America.

Description: Green or brownish; long bodies with papery wings; enlarged front legs adapted for grasping; 2½ inches long. EGGS: White or light brown; masses glued to stems and twigs.

Life Cycle: One generation per year. Winter is passed in the egg stage.

Feeding Habits: Nymphs and adults feed on aphids, beetles, bugs, leafhoppers, flies, bees and wasps, caterpillars, butterflies, and each other.

2½"

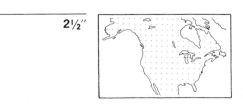

WALKINGSTICK
Walkingstick
Diapheromera femorata

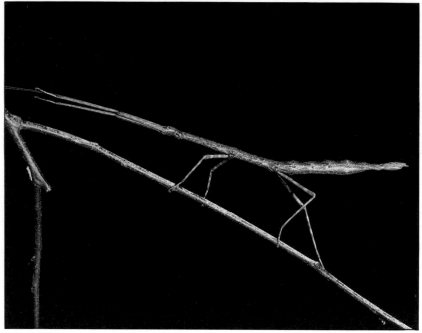

Lemmo / Adult

Range: Eastern United States.

Description: Brown or dark green; thin, sticklike body; easily camouflaged in trees and shrubs; 3 inches long. EGGS: Black, deposited on the ground.

Life Cycle: One generation per year. Winter is passed in the egg stage.

Host Plants: Cherry.

Feeding Habits: Nymphs may feed extensively on foliage, but damage is never serious.

3″

152

EARWIGS

DERMAPTERA

These slender brown insects are often found in the garden, but they rarely pose a serious threat to crops. They are primarily night feeders and spend the day hiding in cracks and crannies, under bark or in plant debris. Most species are scavengers but a few may feed on stems, foliage, and fruits. Some are predaceous.

Earwigs are distinguished by a pair of sharp pincers or forceps on the tip of the abdomen. These are used to grab ants that attack from the rear. Adults have four wings, the front pair being short and leathery. When the insect is at rest, its membranous hind wings are folded up under the front wings.

Eggs are laid in a nest in the soil and watched over by the female. Upon hatching, the nymphs are cared for until they are old enough to make it on their own. Earwigs have incomplete metamorphosis in which they pass through several instars before achieving adulthood.

Control measures are unnecessary for these insects. Although they are hideous in appearance, they do not bite and they do not seriously injure crops. Nor do they enter people's ears, as an old wives' tale suggests.

EARWIG
European Earwig
Forficula auricularia

Badgley / Adult and eggs

Range: Eastern North America with similar species throughout North America.

Description: Reddish brown with short, leathery fore wings; straight and thin with pincers on the tip of the abdomen; ¾ inch long. EGGS: White, round; laid in the soil.

Life Cycle: One to two generations per year. Hibernates in the egg stage.

Host Plants: Many young garden plants and fruit trees.

Feeding Habits: Nymphs feed on plant shoots and eat holes in foliage and flowers. Sometimes ripening fruits are infested, but damage is tolerable.

Insect Predators: Tachinid fly *(Bigonicheta spinipennis)*.

¾″

FLIES

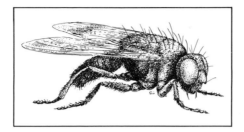

DIPTERA

Many different flies inhabit the garden. In the larval or maggot stages, some are serious pests. They mine between leaf surfaces, tunnel into various roots, or feed within developing fruits. Other species, however, are extremely beneficial to the home gardener. Flower fly larvae feed on aphids and other soft-bodied insects. Tachinid flies parasitize the larvae and pupae of various butterflies and moths, among others. Robber flies capture prey on the wing.

True flies are easily distinguished from other clear-winged insects since they have just one pair of wings. The thorax is generally quite small, the head dominated by two enormous compound eyes, and the legs are clawed. Most species are a dull brown, gray, or black, but a few are bright and shiny. Mouthparts are designed for piercing the plant or animal tissue and lapping or sucking the liquid within.

Flies undergo complete metamorphosis from egg to maggot to pupa to adult. Maggots are usually small, white, legless worms without an obvious head. Their mouthparts are hooked and they tend to feed within their host plant or animal.

Flies are swift, strong fliers sometimes capable of reaching speeds of 30 mph. A special muscle that contracts and recovers instantaneously enables them to beat their wings as much as 1,000 times per second. They exercise precise control in flight, some species being able to hover in one place for long periods. A few can even lay eggs while flying.

To control flies that feed on garden and orchard crops, remove and destroy infested fruits. Apply diatomaceous earth (Perma-Guard) to kill maggots. Eliminate overwintering spots and hiding places by practicing clean cultivation. Resistant varieties of some plants are available and various traps can be purchased to control certain fruit flies.

FLY
Apple Maggot
Rhagoletis pomonella

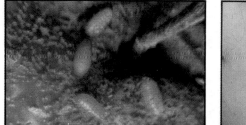

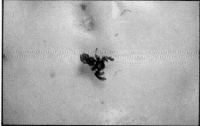

Roberts / Pupae

Kriner / Damage

Badgley / Maggot

Range: Eastern United States and southern Canada.

Description: Black with yellow legs, yellow markings across the abdomen and zigzag bands across the wings; ¼ inch long. EGGS: Laid singly in punctures in the apple skin. LARVA: White or yellowish; ¼ inch long.

Life Cycle: One to two generations per year. Brown pupae hibernate in the soil.

Host Plants: Apple, blueberry, cherry, plum.

Feeding Habits: Adults puncture fruit skin during egg laying. Larvae form winding tunnels within fruit pulp, often causing the entire fruit to rot.

Natural Controls: Trap flies in jars filled with 1 part blackstrap molasses and 9 parts water. Hang in tree branches.

¼"

156

FLY
Cabbage Maggot
Hylemya brassicae

Kriner / Maggots

Oregon / Adult

Range: Western United States.

Description: Gray with black stripes on the thorax; resembles a house fly; ¼ inch long. EGGS: White, laid on plants near the soil surface. LARVA: White; blunt ended; ¼ inch long.

Life Cycle: Two to three broods per year. Winter is passed as a pupa in the soil.

Host Plants: Broccoli, brussels sprouts, cabbage, cauliflower, radish, turnip.

Feeding Habits: Maggots tunnel into roots and stems, causing plants to wilt and develop bacterial or fungal diseases.

Insect Predators: Rove beetles.

Natural Controls: Protect seedlings with a square of tar paper laid flat on the ground around the stem or cover with screening. Dust with rock phosphate or with diatomaceous earth.

¼″

FLY
Carrot Rust Fly
Psila rosae

Oregon / Adult

Range: Throughout most of North America.

Description: Black or green with yellow hair, head, and legs; ⅕ inch long. EGGS: Laid in the crowns of plants. LARVA: Yellow to white; ⅓ inch long.

Life Cycle: Two to three generations per year. Maggots or pupae hibernate in the soil.

Host Plants: Carrot, celery, parsley, parsnip.

Feeding Habits: Larvae chew roots, leaving reddish brown excrement in their tunnels. Injured plants are dwarfed and often infested with soft-rot bacteria. They decompose quickly. Early plantings are particularly susceptible.

Natural Controls: Sprinkle rock phosphate around the base of plants.

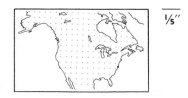

⅕"

FLY
Cherry Fruit Fly/Cherry Maggot
Rhagoletis cingulata

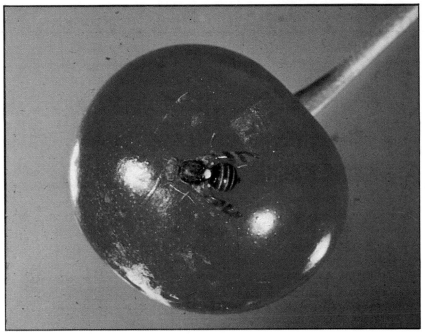

Kriner / Adult

Range: Northern United States and southern Canada.

Description: Black with yellow marks on the thorax, white bands on the abdomen, and dark bands across the wings; shiny; $1/10$ to $1/5$ inch long. EGGS: Yellow; laid in nearly ripe fruits. LARVA: White; $1/4$ inch long.

Life Cycle: One generation per year. Pupae overwinter in the soil.

Host Plants: Cherry, pear, plum.

Feeding Habits: Larvae feed near the center of cherries, causing them to be undersized, misshapen, or decayed. When fully grown they chew their way out of the fruits.

Natural Controls: Spray trees with rotenone as soon as flies appear.

$1/5''$

159

FLY
Currant Fruit Fly
Epochra canadensis

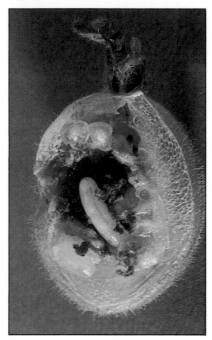

Oregon / Internal damage

Oregon / External damage

Range: United States and southern Canada.

Description: Yellow to dark brown with dark bands on the wings; ⅕ to ⅓ inch long. EGGS: Laid singly in the fruits. LARVA: Yellowish; ⅓ to ½ inch long.

Life Cycle: One brood per year. Winter is passed as a pupa in the soil.

Host Plants: Currant, gooseberry.

Feeding Habits: Maggots feed within developing fruits, causing them to redden and drop prematurely. Injury is greatest to late varieties.

Natural Controls: Dust with rotenone as soon as blossoms wilt, then repeat two to three weeks later.

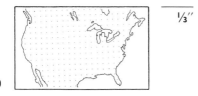

⅓″

FLY
Flower Flies/Hover Flies
Syrphidae

Ross / Adult

Badgley / Larva

Badgley / Adult

Ross / Adult

Range: Various species throughout North America.

Description: Black with yellow bands; hover over flowers and dart away quickly; ⅓ to ½ inch long. EGGS: White; oval; laid singly or in groups on foliage. LARVA: Green to gray or brown; ½ inch long.

Similar Insects: Bees and wasps (pp. 15, 18–19, 22–23).

Life Cycle: Several generations per year. Most species hibernate in the pupal stage.

Feeding Habits: Adults feed on nectar. The larvae of most species feed on aphids, mealybugs, and other small insects.

½″

FLY
Leafminers
Liriomyza sp.

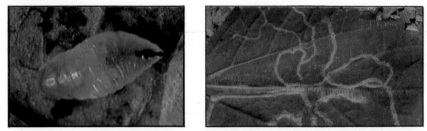

Badgley / Larva   Seip / Damage

Badgley / Adult

Range: Various species throughout North America.

Description: Black with yellow stripes; $1/10$ inch long. EGGS: Laid on leaf surfaces. LARVA: Yellowish; stout; wormlike.

Life Cycle: Several generations per year. Hibernate in cocoons in the soil.

Host Plants: Bean, blackberry, cabbage, lettuce, pepper, potato, spinach, turnip.

Feeding Habits: Maggots mine beneath the surface of leaves, causing white tunnels to form. Related leafminers may chew blotches in leaves.

Natural Controls: Remove and destroy infested leaves.

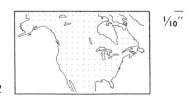

$1/10''$

162

FLY
Mediterranean Fruit Fly
Ceratitis capitata

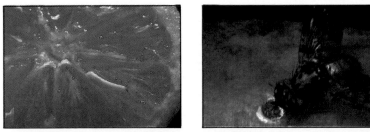

APHIS / Larva

Badgley / Adult

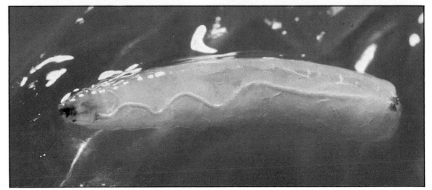

APHIS / Larva

Range: Southern United States.

Description: Black with yellowish marks on the thorax and a yellow abdomen; wings banded with yellow; ¼ inch long. EGGS: White; deposited in holes in fruit rind. LARVA: Whitish; legless; ¼ inch long.

Life Cycle: One to 12 generations per year. Pupae or adults overwinter in the soil or in protected spots.

Host Plants: Many orchard fruit crops.

Feeding Habits: Maggots burrow into fruit pulp, causing it to rot. Although infestations occasionally occur, a government control program has virtually eliminated the insects.

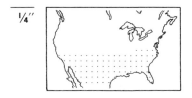

¼"

FLY
Onion Maggot
Hylemya antiqua

Kriner / Adult

Range: Northern United States and southern Canada.

Description: Gray or brown with a humped back and large wings; ¼ inch long. EGGS: White, cylindrical; laid at the base of plants or in bulbs. LARVA: White; blunt ended; ⅓ inch long.

Life Cycle: Two to three generations per year. Hibernates as a pupa in the soil.

Host Plants: Onion.

Feeding Habits: Larvae tunnel into bulbs, ruining crops and often killing young onions. Most damage is done in spring.

Natural Controls: Apply diatomaceous earth to the base of the plants.

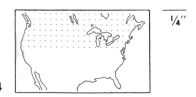

¼"

Pepper Maggot
Zonosemata electa

Kriner / External damage

Kriner / Adult

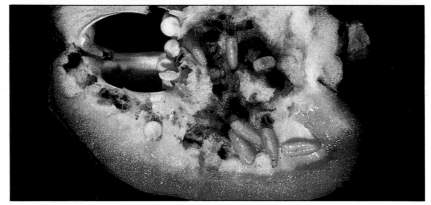

Kriner / Maggots in pepper

Range: Eastern and southwestern United States.

Description: Yellow with brown stripes on the wings; ⅓ inch long. EGGS: White; curved; deposited in developing peppers. LARVA: White to yellow; small; pointed.

Life Cycle: One generation per year. Winter is passed as a pupa in the soil.

Host Plants: Eggplant, pepper, tomato.

Feeding Habits: Maggots feed within peppers, causing them to decay or drop.

Natural Controls: Sprinkle talc, diatomaceous earth, or rock phosphate on the fruits during egg-laying periods. Remove and destroy infested fruits.

⅓″

FLY
Robber Flies
Asilidae

Ross / Adult

Range: Various species throughout North America.

Description: Gray (rarely, yellow and black); a stout beak and hairy mouth; produces a loud buzzing sound; ½ to ¾ inch long. EGGS: Whitish; laid in the soil or on plants. LARVA: White; flat; cylindrical.

Life Cycle: One generation per year, the life cycle requiring at least one year for completion. Most species hibernate as larvae in the soil.

Feeding Habits: Adults capture flying insects such as beetles, leafhoppers, butterflies, flies, and bugs. Larvae prey on white grubs or beetle pupae and sometimes feed on grasshopper eggs.

¾″

FLY
Tachinid Flies
Tachinidae

Badgley / Adult

Ross / Adult

Ross / Adult

Range: Various species throughout North America.

Description: Gray or brown with pale markings; strong flier that walks rapidly on plant surfaces; ⅓ to ½ inch long. EGGS: White; deposited on foliage or on the body of the host. LARVA: Grayish to greenish white; thick bodied; spined.

Life Cycle: Usually many generations per year. Larvae hibernate in the body of the host.

Feeding Habits: Larvae are internal parasites of many beetles, grasshoppers, bugs, caterpillars, and sawflies. They feed within the body of the host, sucking its body fluids and eventually killing the insect.

½″

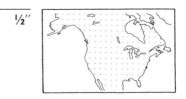

167

FLY
Walnut Husk Fly
Rhagoletis completa

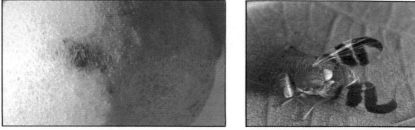

Oregon / External damage   Oregon / Adult

Oregon / Maggots in nut

Range: Western United States with similar species in the East.

Description: Brownish with yellow markings and black bands on the wings and abdomen; ⅓ inch long. EGGS: White; laid in cavities in the husk. LARVA: Yellowish; ½ inch long.

Life Cycle: One generation per year. Pupae overwinter in the soil.

Host Plants: Peach, walnut.

Feeding Habits: Maggots tunnel into the husks, feed for several weeks, then drop to the ground to pupate. Infested nuts are stained, but the kernel remains untouched.

Natural Controls: After harvesting, drop infested nuts into water then remove the drowned maggots along with the husk.

⅓″

LACEWINGS

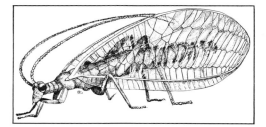

NEUROPTERA

These frail and beautiful insects are among the most interesting and directly beneficial inhabitants of the garden. They possess transparent wings and are active fliers during the cool evening and early morning hours. Often they emit an unpleasant odor, hence their other common name "stinkflies." Brown lacewings (Hemerobiidae) are small with disproportionately large wings. Their body and wings are covered with fine hairs. Green lacewings (Chrysopidae) have slightly larger, smooth bodies, with more delicate features. Larvae and adults of both types feed on aphids and mealybugs.

All lacewings undergo complete metamorphosis. Brown lacewings follow a fairly straightforward life cycle in which eggs are laid on the underside of leaves and hatch into smooth oval, wormlike larvae. These later pupate and become winged adults. Green lacewings, on the other hand, have a slightly different and peculiar life cycle.

When laying her eggs, the female green lacewing touches the tip of her ovipositor to the underside of a leaf where she deposits a tiny pool of clear sticky material. Quickly, she lifts her abdomen and draws the fluid into a long, delicate stalk. It hardens immediately and a small egg is laid upright on the tip. She repeats this process 500 to 600 times until each egg has been placed on a separate thread.

In this way, she lays her eggs in a protected position, inaccessible to ants and other predators. However, she can't protect them from their hatching brothers and sisters. As soon as the larvae have cut their way out of the eggs, they look around for something to eat. Usually the closest living things are neighboring larvae or eggs which they shamelessly pierce and devour. Since eggs are laid where there are plenty of aphids or mealybugs available, the larvae find more acceptable food as soon as they descend their stalks. They are voracious feeders and can consume as many as 60 aphids in one hour and be just as hungry the next hour.

After feeding for several weeks, each larva spins a shining cocoon and rests in the pear-shaped casing for one to two weeks. Then it cuts a hole in the top of the cocoon and slowly crawls from the opening. As an adult, it continues to feed on aphids and mealybugs before entering hibernation.

LACEWING
Antlion / Doodlebug
Hesperoleon abdominalis

Jenkins / Larva

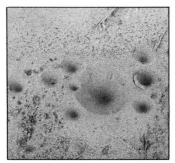

Gossington / Traps

Ross / Adult

Range: Various species throughout North America.

Description: Dark brown with yellow just behind the head; long membranous wings and clubbed antennae; 1½ inches long. EGGS: Laid in sand. LARVA: Brown or grayish; plump abdomen and narrow thorax and head; builds pits; walks backwards.

Life Cycle: One generation per year. Life cycle may require up to two years. Eggs and larvae overwinter in sand.

Feeding Habits: Larvae trap and eat ants and other small insects.

1½″

LACEWING
Green Lacewing
Chrysopa sp.

Lemmo / Adult

Kuhn / Larva

Lemmo / Adult laying eggs and eating aphids

Range: Various species throughout North America.

Description: Pale green; slender body with delicate long green wings; ½ to ¾ inch long. EGGS: White; laid on slender stalks on the underside of leaves. LARVA: Yellowish gray with brown marks; tufts of hair; long jaws.

Life Cycle: Three to four generations per year. Passes the winter in the pupal stage.

Feeding Habits: Many adults and larvae prey on aphids, various larvae, and the eggs of other insects.

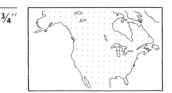
¾"

LEAFHOPPERS, TREEHOPPERS, AND SPITTLEBUGS

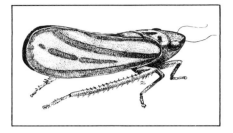

HOMOPTERA

These active insects, along with aphids, cicadas, mealybugs, scales, and whiteflies, belong to the large and diverse order Homoptera. Like their cousins, they are best recognized by the membranous wings which are held rooflike over their body. They are wedge shaped with short antennae and a small head. Mouthparts are similar to those of the true bugs (Hemiptera), but they arise from the back rather than the front part of the head.

Metamorphosis is incomplete with the life cycle often requiring only a few weeks. Females deposit eggs in slits cut in the bark or stems of host plants. Eggs laid in fall spend the winter in their protected spots, then hatch in spring. Many species migrate south in winter, returning north to lay eggs.

Leafhoppers, treehoppers, and spittlebugs are strict vegetarians. In feeding, they extract the juices from plant tissue and inject salivary fluids that begin digesting the food even before it reaches the stomach. The fluids are toxic to plants and they tend to obstruct the plant's nutrient flow. If an unusually large number of leafhoppers are present, plants become stunted and develop discolored leaves. Sometimes the insects transmit viruses that cause Pierce's disease in grape, curly top in the sugar beet, or yellows and other diseases in garden crops.

Although it may seem hard to be enthusiastic over insects that transmit disease and ruin crops, there are some interesting and delightful exceptions in this group. For all their disease-spreading capabilities, *leafhoppers* are seldom present in numbers sufficient to seriously injure plants. They are among the most beautiful animals, marked with bright red, yellow, green, and even blue patterns. When disturbed, the nymphs do a curious sidestepping routine. Some adults are capable of leaping great distances.

Treehoppers are notable for their camouflaging abilities. Massed on the stems and branches of plants, they resemble thorns or tiny bits of bark. They have a large, sculptured hood that extends over the head like the weird helmet of some barbaric knight.

Spittlebugs are similar to the hoppers but much less active when young. During early stages, they simply rest headdown, imbibing cell sap and blowing bubbles. The foam is a mixture of fluid excreted from the anus and a viscous substance produced by special glands. The insect has a pumping chamber beneath its abdomen and, as it draws and expels air, bubbles are formed. Eventually the tiny droplets surround and protect the nymph's entire body.

LEAFHOPPER
Beet Leafhopper
Circulifer tenellus

Badgley / Adult

Range: Western North America with similar species found elsewhere.

Description: Greenish yellow to brown with darker irregular markings; ⅕ inch long. EGGS: Yellowish; deposited in plant stems. NYMPH: Pale green; similar to adult.

Similar Insects: Potato leafhopper (p. 176).

Life Cycle: Several generations per year. Adults hibernate in weeds.

Host Plants: Beet, potato, tomato.

Feeding Habits: Adults and nymphs transmit curly top and tomato yellows, causing plants to be stunted and deformed.

Insect Predators: Bigeyed bugs, some flies, and various wasps.

Natural Controls: Dust plants lightly with diatomaceous earth.

⅕"

LEAFHOPPER
Blue Sharpshooter
Neokolla circellata

Badgley / Adult

Ross / Adults on leaf

Range: Western United States.

Description: Bright green to aqua with blue stripes on the fore wings; active; ⅓ inch long. EGGS: Laid in grass. NYMPH: Resembles adult.

Life Cycle: Three generations per year. Adults hibernate in garden trash.

Host Plants: Grape.

Feeding Habits: Adults and nymphs feed on grape foliage, transmitting Pierce's disease.

Natural Controls: Spray foliage with a forceful jet of water.

⅓"

175

LEAFHOPPER
Potato Leafhopper
Empoasca fabae

Heilman / Damage

Heilman / Adult

Range: Eastern North America.

Description: Green with white spots on the head, wings, and part of the thorax; ⅕ inch long. EGGS: Yellowish white; laid in veins on the underside of leaves.

Similar Insects: Beet leafhopper (p. 174).

Life Cycle: Two to four generations per year. Adults hibernate in garden trash and weeds.

Host Plants: Bean, celery, citrus, eggplant, potato, rhubarb.

Feeding Habits: Adults and nymphs transmit viral diseases to host plants. Infected leaves are curled and stippled or stunted and bleached. Citrus fruit rinds may be punctured or blemished.

Natural Controls: Cover plants with netting in early summer. Diatomaceous earth may control the hoppers.

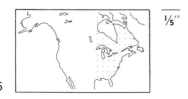

⅕"

LEAFHOPPER
Redbanded Leafhopper
Graphocephala coccinea

Lemmo / Adult

Range: Throughout North America.

Description: Bright green with bands of deep red and green or blue; up to ⅓ inch long.

Life Cycle: One to three generations per year. Adults hibernate in garden trash.

Host Plants: Garden vegetables.

Feeding Habits: Adults and nymphs feed on foliage but they do not cause serious damage.

⅓"

SPITTLEBUG
Spittlebugs/Froghoppers
Cercopidae

Henley / Young adult

Ross / Nymph

Ross / Adult

Range: Various species throughout North America.

Description: Brownish or green, often with stripes or bands on the wings; triangle shaped; ¼ to ⅓ inch long. EGGS: Laid in grasses, between the leaves and main stems. NYMPH: Green; surrounded by masses of froth.

Life Cycle: One generation per year. Winter is passed in the egg stage.

Host Plants: Corn, many garden vegetables and small fruits.

Feeding Habits: Nymphs and adults may feed on some plants, but they are harmless.

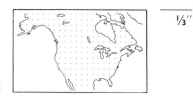

⅓″

TREEHOPPER
Buffalo Treehopper
Stictocephala bubalus

Ross / Adult

Lemmo / Adult

Range: Throughout North America.

Description: Green; a hard, triangular hood covering the head and part of the abdomen; ¼ inch long. EGGS: Yellow; laid in C-shaped slits in bark. NYMPH: Light green; spined.

Life Cycle: One generation per year. Eggs overwinter in bark and hatch the following spring.

Host Plants: Most fruit trees, potato, tomato.

Feeding Habits: Egg slits may seriously injure young fruit trees. Infested trees are scaly, cracked, and dwarfed.

Natural Controls: Apply dormant-oil spray in early spring or dust foliage with diatomaceous earth.

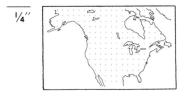

¼"

MEALYBUGS

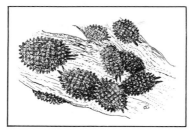

HOMOPTERA

Male mealybugs resemble tiny flies, but the wingless females whose bodies are covered with powdery wax can be easily mistaken for some strange growth. Feeding on stems, leaves, and fruits, their compact colonies look like masses of moldy cotton.

Aside from their strange appearance, mealybugs are really not very different from their small homopteran cousins, the aphids, psyllids, and phylloxera. They suck the juices from plants and spread diseases. The honeydew they secrete invites the growth of a sooty fungus which interferes with photosynthesis. Ants "milk" them, carry them from plant to plant, and protect them from their many natural enemies.

Some mealybugs bear live young. Others lay hundreds of eggs in soft, white sacs that may be as large as the female herself. After depositing them, the female dies. Eggs hatch within two to three weeks and, shortly after, the active yellow nymphs emerge from their egg sac. They begin feeding immediately, sucking plant sap and secreting honeydew. Gradually, the waxy coating begins to form on their bodies and the insects grow sluggish. Females molt twice before entering adulthood. Males generally have an additional pupal period spent in a thin cocoon before they develop into winged adults. They have no mouths and are really nothing more than flying sperm banks, their only purpose being to find and fertilize wingless females.

In the South, the life cycle takes about a month with some variation depending upon temperature and species. Fewer species of mealybug are present in the North, most being tropical or greenhouse insects.

A number of parasites and predators control mealybugs in the garden. Lady beetles, particularly the mealybug destroyer *(Cryptolaemus montrouzieri)*, feed on them. Green lacewing larvae also eat them and have the distinct advantage of working at much lower temperatures than the mealybug destroyer. A parasite, *Leptomastix dactylopii*, is effective in controlling citrus mealybug if the temperature is high enough.

If predators do not take care of the insects, a nontoxic spray such as summer white oil, nicotine sulfate, or nicotine sulfate and summer white oil may work.

MEALYBUG
Citrus Mealybug
Planococcus citri

Badgley / Adults

Range: Southern United States and California.

Description: Yellowish; covered with dense white powder; short, irregular filaments of equal length around the body; $\frac{1}{10}$ inch long.

Life Cycle: Two to three generations per year. Winter is passed in the egg stage.

Host Plants: Avocado, citrus, potato.

Feeding Habits: Adults and nymphs feed on cell sap in twigs and foliage.

Insect Predators: Mealybug destroyer.

Natural Controls: Spray fruit trees with water, soapy water, or kerosene emulsion.

$\overline{\qquad}$
$\frac{1}{10}''$

MEALYBUG
Comstock Mealybug
Pseudococcus comstocki

Roberts / Damage   Badgley / Adult

Range: Eastern United States and California. Other species throughout North America.

Description: White; elliptically shaped with short waxy spines; ¼ inch long. EGGS: Laid under bark.

Host Plants: Apple, grape, peach, pear.

Feeding Habits: Infested fruits are disfigured and may be covered with dark mold. Branches are infested near pruning scars, causing galls to form.

Insect Predators: Various chalcid wasps control the insects on grape.

Natural Controls: Spray foliage with water or soapy water.

¼″

183

MEALYBUG
Longtailed Mealybug
Pseudococcus adonidum

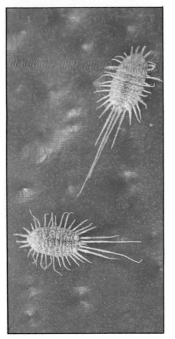

Badgley / Adults

Badgley / Adults and eggs

Range: Throughout North America, particularly in the South.

Description: White, waxy, and cottony with very long anal filaments; young are born live; $^1/_{10}$ inch long.

Life Cycle: Many generations per year. Winter is passed in all stages.

Host Plants: Avocado, banana, citrus, plum.

Feeding Habits: Mealybugs feed on fruits, foliage, and stems.

Insect Predators: Several chalcid wasps *(Anarhopus sydneyensis, Hungariella peregrina).*

Natural Controls: Spray plants with water or soapy water.

$\overline{}^1/_{10}''$

PSYLLIDS

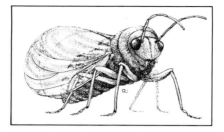

HOMOPTERA

Psyllids, or jumping plant lice, are similar to aphids but have long antennae and strong legs adapted for jumping. Clear winged, they resemble minute cicadas that hop or fly away when disturbed. The wingless nymphs may be easily confused with woolly aphids since they produce large amounts of a white, cottony substance.

Psyllids feed on a variety of plants, including most fruit trees and small fruits, as well as potato and tomato. Like aphids, they pierce leaf surfaces with their small beaks and extract the cell sap. This causes foliage to turn yellow, curl, and eventually to die. Sometimes galls are formed. Honeydew secreted by the psyllids attracts other insects and encourages the growth of dark sooty molds. Many species transmit disease-carrying viruses.

Metamorphosis is incomplete, but the life histories vary among the many species. Some psyllids hibernate as adults, emerging in spring to lay eggs. Others overwinter in the egg stage. There are several generations per year.

Although they are potentially serious pests capable of defoliating an entire orchard, psyllids rarely cause much direct damage. Their eggs provide food for many birds and larger insects. Healthy plants can usually support a small psyllid population without suffering any serious injuries.

The real problems are caused by the viruses and molds that form on the sticky leaves and fruits. Blossoms shrivel and rot and fruit is ruined. A dormant-oil spray applied to hardy trees in early spring will suffocate the insects as they hatch from eggs and will help to limit their numbers.

PSYLLID
Pear Psylla
Psylla pyricola

Kriner / Nymph

Kriner / Adult

Range: Eastern United States and the Pacific Northwest. Similar species distributed elsewhere.

Description: Reddish brown with green or red markings; transparent wings; 1/10 inch long. EGGS: Yellowish; laid at the base of buds, on twigs, or on the upper surfaces of leaves near the veins.

Life Cycle: Three to five generations per year. Adults hibernate in garden litter.

Host Plants: Pear, quince; similar species attack potato, tomato.

Feeding Habits: Nymphs and adults feed on foliage and fruits, excreting honeydew which encourages the growth of sooty mold. Infested leaves develop brown spots; fruits are scarred; buds may fail to develop.

Insect Predators: Chalcid wasp *(Trechnites insidiosus)*.

Natural Controls: Spray trees with dormant oil in the spring or, if they are well established, dust with limestone or diatomaceous earth.

1/10"

SCALES

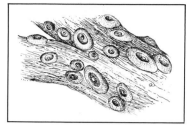

HOMOPTERA

Scales are such oddly shaped and immobile insects that, like mealybugs, they resemble disease organisms more closely than animals. Members of the superfamily Coccidea, they attach themselves to the leaves, fruits, and bark of many different plants. They suck plant juices and sometimes cause considerable damage.

There are two families of scales: *Soft scales* (Coccidea) that tend to feed on garden crops, and the *armored scales* (Diaspididae) that prefer orchard crops. Their life cycles vary from species to species, but all follow some complex variation of incomplete metamorphosis.

Soft scales are usually covered with a waxy or cottony substance secreted by their bodies. Males may have no wings or they may possess a single pair of translucent wings. They are usually more mobile than the females who, in the adult stage, lack both legs and wings. Females are flat and long, often with a hard exoskeleton or waxy coating. Like aphids, they can give birth to live nymphs as well as lay eggs. Eggs are deposited in soft cottony sacs or beneath scales. The young nymphs are known as crawlers. They have legs and antennae and are very active as first instars. Black *(Saissetia oleae)* and cottonycushion *(Icerya purchasi)* scales are common members of this family.

Armored scales possess a much stronger coating which they make from their waxy secretions and cast-off skins. Round armored scales, such as San Jose *(Quadraspidiotus perniciosus)* and California red *(Aonidiella aurantii)*, enlarge their armor by adding fine threads of wax to the outer edges while rotating their bodies. More elongate species such as oystershell scale *(Lepidosaphes ulmi)* rock their bodies from side to side as the wax is added. These armors are then used as protection and as safe places to lay eggs. Their size, color, and shape differ according to species.

Armored scales have a life cycle similar to that of soft scales. Young are born alive or hatch from eggs and are active until the first molt. Adult females lack eyes, legs, and antennae. Males are winged with well-developed antennae and simple eyes.

A number of insects prey on scales and play an important role in controlling them in the garden and orchard. Various lady beetles, parasitic aphids, and chalcid wasps are particularly beneficial.

Dormant-oil sprays applied before buds open, help control the insects in the orchard. Soapy water sprayed over them often kills young ones. They can be scraped from tree limbs and branches.

SCALE
California Red Scale
Aonidiella aurantii

 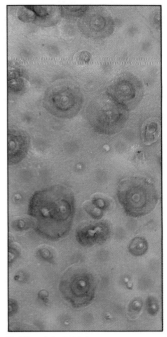

Badgley / Infested fruit   Badgley / Infested fruit

Range: Southern United States.

Description: Reddish brown; tortoise shaped with a small nipple at the center of the caplike covering; 1/12 inch long. NYMPH: Brown; borne live, move about for several hours before beginning to feed.

Life Cycle: Many broods. Winter is passed in all stages.

Host Plants: Citrus, fig, grape, walnut.

Feeding Habits: Scales feed on all parts of trees, including fruits. They inject a toxic substance, causing leaves and fruits to develop yellow spots. Citrus is particularly susceptible to serious injuries.

Insect Predators: Various chalcid wasps (*Aphytis lingnanensis, A. melinus,* and *Prospaltella perniciosi*).

Natural Controls: Apply a dormant-oil spray in early spring.

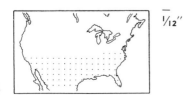

1/12"

SCALE
Cottonycushion Scale
Icerya purchasi

Badgley / Colony

Range: Southern United States.

Description: Reddish brown; females covered with a white, ridged mass that holds up to 800 red eggs; ⅕ inch long. NYMPH: Red with black legs, antennae, and long hair.

Life Cycle: Three generations per year. Winter is passed in all stages.

Host Plants: Almond, apple, apricot, citrus, fig, peach, pecan, pepper, potato, quince, walnut.

Feeding Habits: Scales attach themselves to stems and bark.

Insect Predators: Many lady beetles, particularly vedalia.

Natural Controls: Spray with dormant oil early in spring, before growth begins.

⅕"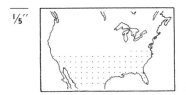

SCALE
Purple Scale
Lepidosaphes beckii

Badgley / Adult and pupae

Ross / Infested fruit

Range: Southern United States.

Description: Purplish or brown armor; oystershell shaped; $1/12$ inch long. EGGS: White; laid in groups of 50 beneath the female's shell. NYMPH: Whitish with brown tip; covered with cottony wax until armor forms.

Life Cycle: Two to three generations per year. Winter is passed in all stages.

Host Plants: Citrus.

Feeding Habits: Scales feed on all plant parts, injecting a toxic substance that kills leaves and branches.

Natural Controls: Spray with summer-oil spray.

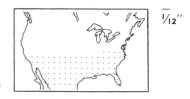
$1/12''$

SCALE
San Jose Scale
Quadraspidiotus perniciosus

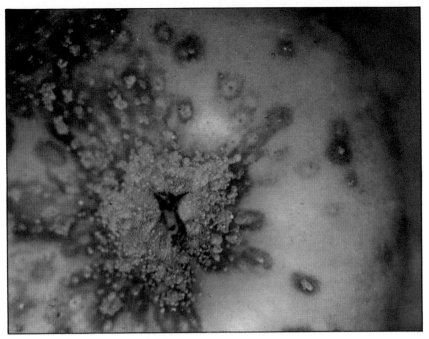

Jenkins / Infested apple

Range: United States and southern Canada.

Description: Grayish with a dark projection in the center and small yellow pouches beneath. NYMPH: Yellow; borne live.

Life Cycle: Up to six generations per year. Dark nymphs overwinter on bark.

Host Plants: Apple, cherry, peach, pear, pecan, quince.

Feeding Habits: Compact colonies feed on bark and fruits, often causing a red, inflamed area to form around them. If left unchecked, trees may die.

Natural Controls: Spray with dormant oil in early spring, just before blossoms open.

$\frac{1}{12}''$

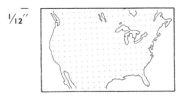

THRIPS

THYSANOPTERA

There is no such thing as one thrip. The word "thrips" is both singular and plural and, since one thrips is inevitably followed by another, the singular form is rarely used.

Thrips are a gregarious lot. They congregate by the hundreds on flowers and leaves. Without the aid of a hand lens, they resemble tiny dark threads. A closer look reveals their narrow, fringed wings folded flat on the back and cone-shaped mouthparts. Extremely active insects, they leap and fly away when disturbed. If not in any particular hurry, they may crawl with the abdomen lifted and perhaps curved over their backs.

Most thrips are plant-eaters. To feed, they scrape the epidermal layer of the host plant, then suck the cell sap as it flows into the wound. Some species may burrow between the upper and lower leaf surfaces to feed. Blossoms become streaked with brown and wither prematurely. Injured leaves are twisted or discolored and scarred. The fruit of host plants is often pitted.

A few species are beneficial predators of mites, small insects, and other thrips. Most of these can be distinguished by their banded or mottled wings.

Metamorphosis in this order is incomplete with the nymph passing through four instars. Eggs are inserted in leaves and stems. One to two weeks later, nymphs emerge and begin to feed. During the first three stages, the pale wingless young feed actively but in the final period, they are entirely quiescent. Some species form a cocoon on the ground or on the host plant at this time.

Many generations may occur each year, but largest populations are present from late spring to midsummer. Yet, even during this period, thrips seldom cause serious damage to their host. Their worst effect is russeting or, in the case of citrus thrips, early blossom drop. If the problem becomes serious and the numbers justify it, tobacco dust may be used to control them.

THRIPS
Citrus Thrips
Scirtothrips citri

Badgley / Nymphs

Ross / Adults

Range: Southwestern United States.

Description: Brownish orange with dark hood and abdominal margins, similar species black; 1/50 inch long. EGGS: Kidney shaped; thrust into young leaves, stems, twigs, or fruits. NYMPH: Yellowish orange with red eyes.

Life Cycle: Many generations per year, a new one emerging every two or three weeks. Overwinters in the egg stage, except in the warmest regions where it breeds year-round.

Host Plants: Citrus, date, grape, peach.

Feeding Habits: Thrips suck juices from plant tissue, causing flowers to become streaked with brown and wither prematurely. Fruit develops a ring around the blossom end.

Natural Controls: Apply a dust of sulfur or diatomaceous earth if the thrips are truly injuring fruit crops. Usually this is unnecessary.

1/50"

WEEVILS

COLEOPTERA

Weevils are beetles whose mouthparts are attached to the end of a beak or snout. Those with a particularly long or pronounced and curved snout are sometimes called *curculios*. Garden species are mostly small, dull colored, and hard shelled.

Adults are potential plant pests, but usually larvae cause the most serious injury. They feed on fruits, nuts, and plant roots. Eggs are laid in or on the plant where larval feeding will occur. Larvae feed and pupate within the plant, emerging later to lay eggs. There may be several generations per year, depending upon the species.

A few weevils are bound to turn up in most fruit and root crops. This is to be expected and does not mean that the entire crop has "failed." But, if weevil populations do get out of hand, you may find it necessary to shorten their life cycle. Pick up dropped fruit and bury it very deep. Eliminate the insects' hibernating spots in garden trash and the upper inches of the soil. Since weevils tend to drop from trees and bushes when disturbed, you can collect them throughout the summer by placing a sheet beneath the infested tree and shaking the branches. If these control measures fail, dust foliage with diatomaceous earth (Perma-Guard).

WEEVIL
Apple Curculio
Tachypterellus quadrigibbus

Heilman / Damage

Jenkins / Adult

Range: Eastern North America.

Description: Brownish red; humped with a long snout; $\frac{1}{10}$ inch long. EGGS: Laid in punctures placed close together on the fruit surface. LARVA: White or grayish; wormlike.

Similar Insects: Plum curculio (p. 201).

Life Cycle: One generation per year. Adults hibernate in sheltered spots.

Host Plants: Apple, pear, quince.

Feeding Habits: Larvae feed and pupate in fallen fruit or injured fruit still on the tree.

Natural Controls: Shake branches and collect curculios as they fall on a sheet below or dust with diatomaceous earth.

$\overline{\frac{1}{10}''}$

WEEVIL
Bean Weevil
Acanthoscelides obtectus

Badgley / Adult

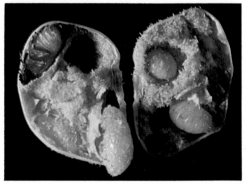

Badgley / Infestation

Badgley / Eggs

Badgley / Larvae and pupa

Range: Throughout North America.

Description: Brown or dark green with darker mottling; flat; $\frac{1}{10}$ to $\frac{1}{5}$ inch long. EGGS: White; laid on beans. LARVA: Whitish.

Life Cycle: Outdoors, one brood per season; in stored beans, weevils breed continuously. Outdoors, adults hibernate under garden trash.

Host Plants: Bean, pea.

Feeding Habits: Many larvae feed within each bean seed, pupate, then emerge through a small hole.

Natural Controls: Dry seed after harvesting.

$\frac{1}{5}''$

WEEVIL
Cabbage Curculio
Ceutorhynchus rapae

Oregon / Adult

Range: Throughout North America.

Description: Black with bluish or yellowish hair; a curved, slender beak with antennae in the middle; ⅛ inch long. EGGS: Gray; oval; inserted in plant stems. LARVA: Whitish.

Life Cycle: Several generations per year. Adults hibernate in the soil.

Host Plants: Broccoli, cabbage, cauliflower, turnip.

Feeding Habits: Adults and grubs mine stalks and feed on leaves, but controls are seldom necessary.

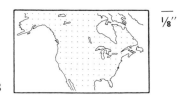

⅛"

WEEVIL
Carrot Weevil
Listronotus oregonensis

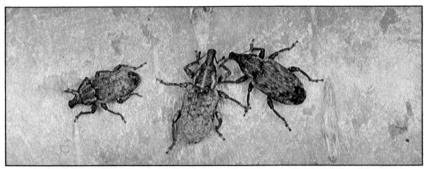

Jenkins / Adults

Jenkins / Larva and damage

Range: Eastern and central North America.

Description: Dark brown to coppery; hard shelled; ⅕ inch long. EGGS: White; deposited in the stalks of leaves. LARVA: White with brown head; curved; legless.

Similar Insects: Vegetable weevil (p. 203).

Life Cycle: Two generations per year. Adult beetles overwinter in grass and garden litter.

Host Plants: Carrot, celery, dill, parsley.

Feeding Habits: Grubs mine into the tops of carrot roots or into celery hearts. Their zigzag paths destroy much of the plant's tissue.

Natural Controls: Crop rotation and cultivation are the only effective organic controls.

⅕″

WEEVIL
Pecan Weevil
Curculio caryae

Clemson / Adult

Range: Southern United States.

Description: Dark brown with short yellow hair; a beak almost as long as the body; ¼ inch long. EGGS: White; laid in small punctures in the nuts. LARVA: Whitish.

Life Cycle: One generation per year, the life cycle requiring two to three years. Larvae spend the winter in cells in the soil.

Host Plants: Pecan.

Feeding Habits: Larvae chew nut kernels, later emerging through a hole in the shell.

Natural Controls: Pick up and destroy dropped nuts. Shake tree branches and gather weevils that fall on the sheet below. Diatomaceous earth applied as a dust helps control the insects before they enter nuts.

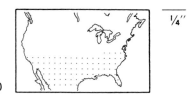

¼"

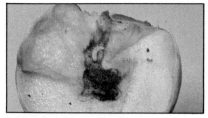

Jenkins / Larva

Clemson / Larva

Jenkins / Adults

Range: Eastern North America.

Description: Dark brown with fine, white hair on the body; sculptured wing covers; slightly curved, thick beak; ¼ inch long. EGGS: White to gray; elliptical; laid beneath crescent-shaped slits in the skin of fruits.

Similar Insects: Apple curculio (p. 196).

Life Cycle: One to two generations per year. Adults hibernate in the soil.

Host Plants: Apple, blueberry, cherry, peach, pear, plum, quince.

Feeding Habits: Adults damage fruits during egg laying. Larvae mine within fruits for several weeks before leaving to pupate in the soil. Brown rot develops, causing fruits to be deformed or to drop prematurely.

Natural Controls: Knock weevils from the trees onto a sheet. Pick up and destroy dropped fruits.

¼"

WEEVIL
Rhubarb Curculio
Lixus concavus

Jenkins / Adult

Range: United States.

Description: Brown or black with grayish hairs; often covered with orange pollen; ½ inch long. EGGS: Laid in punctures in stalks. LARVA: Whitish.

Life Cycle: One generation per year. Adults hibernate in weeds.

Host Plants: Rhubarb.

Feeding Habits: Larvae feed on dock, sunflower, and related plants; adults may damage rhubarb during egg laying.

Natural Controls: Curculios are easily controlled by handpicking.

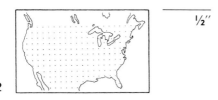

½"

WEEVIL
Vegetable Weevil
Listroderes costirostris obliquus

Clemson / Adult

Oregon / Egg

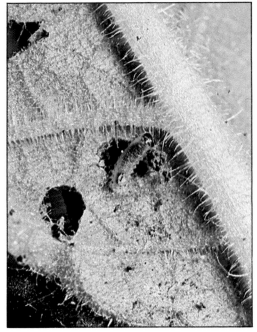

Clemson / Larva

Range: Southern United States.

Description: Gray to brownish with a lighter V-shaped mark near the tip of the wing covers; ½ inch long. EGGS: Laid on stems and crowns of plants. LARVA: Greenish; sluglike; ¼ inch long.

Similar Insects: Carrot weevil (p. 199).

Life Cycle: One generation per year. Adults pass the winter sheltered by garden litter and weeds.

Host Plants: Beet, cabbage, carrot, lettuce, onion, potato, radish, spinach, tomato, turnip.

Feeding Habits: Grubs and adults begin feeding on the crown, then chew foliage, leaving only stems.

Natural Controls: Dust plants with a small amount of diatomaceous earth.

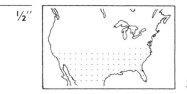

½″

WHITEFLIES

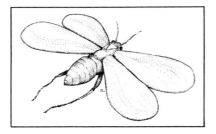

HOMOPTERA

In the South, these tiny, mothlike insects are often present in large numbers on the underside of leaves. They may go unnoticed unless the plant is disturbed and they fly off in great clouds. Adults are about $\frac{1}{20}$ inch long with two pairs of soft wings covered with a waxy white powder.

Metamorphosis is incomplete, but it differs somewhat from that of most other members of the order Homoptera. Minute eggs, about $\frac{1}{100}$ inch long, are laid on stalks attached to the underside of leaves. These hatch into active six-legged yellowish nymphs which thrust their beaks into plant tissue and begin extracting cell sap. Subsequent instars are much less active. During the first molt, nymphs lose their antennae and legs. They resemble small, flat scales covered with waxy threads. In the stages that follow, nymphs begin to develop wings internally, but they change very little in outward appearance. In the second to last stage, they stop feeding and rest in a sort of pupal state before molting for the last time and emerging as full-fledged, winged adults. Females have legs, but males remain legless.

In all stages, whiteflies secrete honeydew. Most of the problems caused by the insects are associated with this secretion. Since they are primarily tropical insects, they usually infest garden plants only in warm climates which tend to favor the growth of a dark, sooty fungus. Fruits become pale in color and are stunted. Foliage is yellowish and very dry.

A small parasite, *Encarsia formosa,* helps control whiteflies in greenhouses and may even be useful in the garden. Adult females lay eggs in the whitefly nymphs and pupae. Eggs hatch and, as the larvae develop, their hosts blacken and die. Parasitized whiteflies look like specks of pepper on the leaves.

WHITEFLY
Greenhouse Whitefly
Trialeurodes vaporariorum

Kuhn / Adults and eggs

Range: Southern and coastal United States.

Description: White; covered with a powdery substance; mothlike; $\frac{1}{20}$ to $\frac{1}{12}$ inch long. EGGS: Yellow; cone shaped; laid on small projections on the underside of leaves. NYMPH: Green, translucent; flat, with fine waxy filaments.

Life Cycle: Many broods each year. Hibernates in the nymph stage.

Host Plants: Most fruits and vegetables.

Feeding Habits: Nymphs and adults suck the juices from succulent new growth and cause plants to become weak and susceptible to disease.

Natural Controls: Dust with tobacco dust or spray with tobacco tea.

$\overline{}^{1}/_{12}''$

WIREWORMS

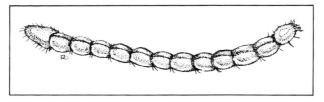

COLEOPTERA

These long, cylindrical worms with their tough, shiny skin are the larvae of a beetle. Usually, they are reddish brown in color but first instars may be paler with a softer skin. They grow up to 1½ inches long and have three pairs of legs just behind the head. Unlike millipedes or thousand-leggers which they resemble, wireworms do not curl up into a loose spiral position when disturbed. They feed entirely underground, chewing on germinating seeds or on the roots, stems, and tubers of many plants.

In their adult stage, wireworms are known as click beetles (Elateridae). These beetles are notable for their ability to click and right themselves when placed on their backs. By bending back the head and hood area of the thorax, the beetle curls its body so that only its legs are touching the ground. Then, with a sudden jerk, it straightens its body, causing the wing covers and hood to strike the ground. This flips the beetle into the air. If the process is repeated often enough, the insect finally lands upright.

As with other beetles, metamorphosis in this group is complete. Eggs are laid underground in early spring or summer and pupation takes place in late summer. Many species require several years to develop. They pass the winter in the soil or in rotten wood or plant debris.

If wireworms are a problem on your property, try growing resistant crops. Cultivate the garden frequently enough to expose the worms to enemies and to discourage egg laying, but not so often that erosion becomes a problem. Traps, such as pieces of potato buried an inch below the soil surface, attract the larvae and can be removed periodically.

WIREWORM
Eastern Field Wireworm
Limonius agonus

Ross / Larva

Range: Eastern North America. Similar species throughout North America.

Description: Brown to yellowish; shiny, hard skin; cylindrical; ⅓ to ½ inch long. ADULT: Black to grayish or brown with dark spots on the head and bands across the wing covers; ½ inch long. EGGS: Laid in damp soil several inches beneath the surface.

Similar Insects: Millipedes (p. 211).

Life Cycle: One generation per year, the life cycle requiring one to six years to complete. Adult beetles overwinter in cells in the soil.

Host Plants: Bean, beet, carrot, corn, lettuce, onion, pea, potato.

Feeding Habits: Larvae chew seed, feed on underground roots and tubers, and burrow into other plant parts.

Natural Controls: Trap wireworms in pieces of potato scattered around the garden.

½″

NON-INSECTS

There are a number of small creatures in the garden that crawl about as insects, feed as insects, and even resemble insects, but when you look closely, you realize they are obviously *not* insects. Some belong to a different class in the phylum Arthropoda while others, lacking a segmented body or hard exoskeleton, are members of an entirely different phylum.

Centipedes are close relatives of insects. They have antennae, they breathe through spiracles and a system of branched tubes, they have a distinct head and jointed legs. But, they have only two body parts, no wings and, instead of six legs, they have 30 or more. Therefore they are members of the class Chilopoda, not Insecta.

Millipedes with up to 400 legs are also close relatives of insects that make up an entirely different class, Diplopoda. They live in the soil and feed primarily on dead plant material, although they will occasionally eat roots, tubers, and fruits.

Sow bugs or *pill bugs* are those familiar grayish brown creatures that roll into a ball when disturbed. They cannot be classified as insects because their bodies are not divided into three distinct segments and because they breathe through gills, not spiracles. They tend to live in damp, protected places, beneath old boards or in compost.

Mites are the smallest creatures you can actually see in the garden. If you were to look at one under a microscope, you would see that they have four pairs of legs, no antennae, and no thorax. They resemble tiny ticks and, with those insects, belong to the class Arachnida.

Slugs and *snails* are the largest soil-dwelling creatures that might be mistaken for insects. They tend to feed on plants and they have tiny projections that roughly resemble antennae, but, since they are soft bodied without legs at any time in their life cycle, they are classed in a separate phylum, Mollusca.

NON-INSECT
Garden Symphylan/Garden Centipede
Class: Chilopoda

Kriner / Adult

Range: Throughout North America.

Description: White; flat; 12 legged with long antennae; active; ¼ inch long. EGGS: White; laid in clusters 1 foot deep in the soil.

Life Cycle: Many generations per year. Winter is spent in the adult stage in the soil.

Host Plants: Asparagus, cucumber, lettuce, radish, tomato.

Feeding Habits: Symphylans sever small roots and scar underground plant parts. Plants become stunted and may even die.

Natural Controls: Flooding may control them or try a tobacco infusion poured into the soil.

¼″

NON-INSECT
Millipedes
Class: Diplopoda

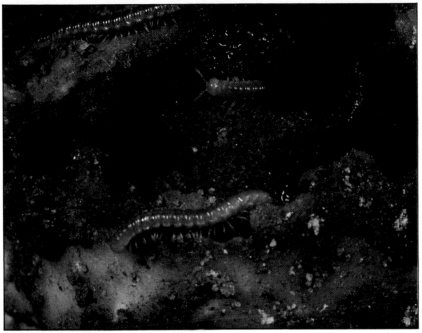

Badgley / Adults in potato

Range: Throughout North America.

Description: Brown to pinkish brown or gray; long, round wormlike body with many segments and two or more legs per segment; found coiled like a spring; ½ inch long. EGGS: Translucent; sticky; laid in clusters in or on the soil.

Similar Insects: Eastern field wireworm (p. 208).

Life Cycle: One generation per year. Winter is passed in the soil.

Host Plants: Bean, cabbage, carrot, corn, potato, strawberry, tomato, turnip.

Feeding Habits: Most species feed on decayed plant material but they may eat plant roots or enter fruits and tubers in or on damp soil. Seedlings are often severed. Fungal diseases attack larger plants. Some millipedes are predators that eat many kinds of soil insects.

Natural Controls: Drench infested soil with tobacco tea if millipedes become a problem.

½"

NON-INSECT
Mites/Spider Mites
Class: Arachnida

Kriner / Adult

Clemson / Damage

Clemson / Damage

Range: Throughout North America.

Description: Reddish brown or pale in color; spiderlike with eight legs and no antennae, thorax, or wings; about $1/150$ to $1/50$ inch long. EGGS: Laid at the base of plants or on leaves and buds.

Life Cycle: Many generations per year, the life cycle often requiring only a few days. Adult mites hibernate in debris or under bark.

Host Plants: Various species feed on many plants, particularly fruit trees and various small fruits. European red mites are a major problem on apple trees in the Northeast. They are most common in warm regions.

Feeding Habits: Mites feed on leaves, fruits, and roots. Infested leaves become silvery and may turn yellow. They curl and may be covered with a fine web. Fruit may be russeted, dry, and rough or deformed. A few species of mites form blisters on young leaves.

Insect Predators: Lacewings, lady beetles, predatory mites.

Natural Controls: Spray cold water on leaves or try a slurry of wheat flour, buttermilk, and water.

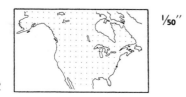

$1/50''$

NON-INSECT
Slugs and Snails
Phylum: Mollusca

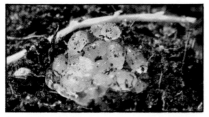
Gossington / Snail eggs

Gossington / Predaceous snail

Heilman / Slug

Range: Various species throughout North America.

Description: Gray to black or brown; soft bodied, often with a soft hump in the center; eyes at the tips of small tentacles; two other tentacles used for smelling. Snails have a single shell; slugs have none; ½ to 3 inches long.

Life Cycle: Several years are required to complete the life cycle. Winter is spent in the soil or in garden litter.

Host Plants: Many garden and orchard crops.

Feeding Habits: Most slugs and snails feed at night, spending the day beneath decaying boards or in garden trash. They scrape holes in foliage and may cause extensive damage. Some snail species are predaceous and feed on many different small insects.

Natural Controls: Handpick slugs and snails when they emerge in the evenings. Place shallow saucers of stale beer in the garden and collect the slugs as they drown in them. Dust with diatomaceous earth for more serious infestations.

3″

Insect Damage to Foliage

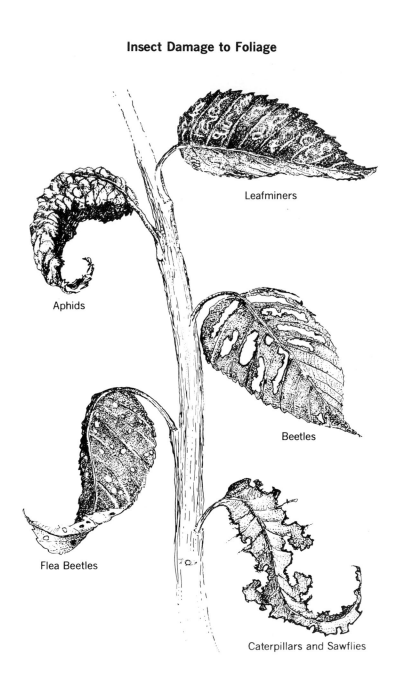

Leafminers

Aphids

Beetles

Flea Beetles

Caterpillars and Sawflies

Insect Damage to Fruit

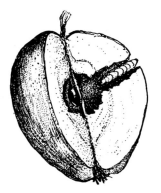

Caterpillars

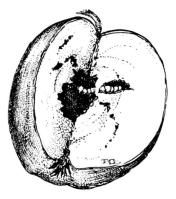

Maggots

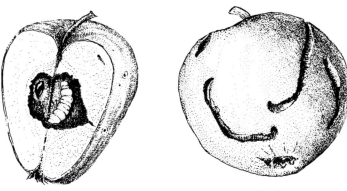

Weevils

Sawflies

APPENDIX: Common Fruits and Vegetables and the Insects That Feed on Them

CROP	FOLIAGE	FLOWERS AND FRUITS	STEMS AND BRANCHES	ROOTS
Almond	Aphids Beetles: flea, striped blister Bugs: boxelder Caterpillars: fruittree leafroller, omnivorous looper, redhumped, western tent Leafhoppers Noninsects: mites Scales	Aphids Caterpillars: navel orangeworm Thrips	Aphids Borers: California prionus	
Apple	Aphids Beetles: fig, flea, grape colaspis, green June, Japanese Bugs: apple red, boxelder Caterpillars: apple-and-thorn skeletonizer, eastern tent, fall cankerworm, fall webworm, forest tent, fruittree leafroller, gypsy moth, obliquebanded leafroller, redbanded leafroller, spring cankerworm, walnut, western tent, western tussock moth Cicadas Crickets: snowy tree Leafhoppers Mealybugs Noninsects: mites Psyllids Scales	Aphids Beetles: fig, green June, Japanese Bugs: apple red, green stink Caterpillars: codling moth, eyespotted bud moth, green fruitworm, oriental fruit moth Flies: apple maggot Mealybugs: comstock Scales Thrips Wasps: European apple sawfly Weevils	Borers: California prionus, flatheaded appletree, roundheaded appletree, shothole	Aphids Wireworms
Apricot *See Peach*				
Asparagus	Aphids Beetles: asparagus, Japanese, spotted asparagus, spotted cucumber Bugs: harlequin, Say stink Caterpillars: cutworms, orange tortrix, yellow woollybear			

Asparagus (CONT.)	Leafminers Noninsects: centipedes Scales			
Avocado	Aphids Beetles: flea, June Bugs: harlequin, lace Caterpillars: cutworms, omnivorous looper, orange tortrix Crickets: snowy tree Noninsects: mites Scales Whiteflies	Mealybugs: citrus, longtailed Thrips	Borers: shothole	
Bean	Aphids Beetles: bean leaf, flea, grape colaspis, June, Mexican bean, spotted cucumber, striped blister, striped cucumber, whitefringed Borers: European corn Bugs: green stink, harlequin, leaffooted, Say stink, tarnished plant Caterpillars: corn earworm, cutworms, fall armyworm, gray hairstreak, green cloverworm Mealybugs Noninsects: mites Whiteflies	Borers Thrips Weevils: bean, cowpea	Borers	Aphids Noninsects: millipedes
Beet	Aphids Beetles: flea, spotted cucumber, striped blister, striped cucumber Borers: European corn Caterpillars: cabbage looper, cutworms, yellow woollybear Leafhoppers Leafminers Thrips			Aphids Beetles: carrot, flea Flies: cabbage maggot Thrips Weevils: vegetable Wireworms

CROP	FOLIAGE	FLOWERS AND FRUITS	STEMS AND BRANCHES	ROOTS
Blackberry **See Raspberry**				
Blueberry	Beetles: flea, green June Caterpillars: fall webworm, yellownecked Leafhoppers: spittlebugs Leafminers Noninsects: mites Scales Thrips	Flies Thrips Weevils: plum curculio		
Boysenberry **See Raspberry**				
Broccoli **See Cabbage**				
Brussels **Sprouts** **See Cabbage**				
Cabbage	Aphids Beetles: flea, margined blister, spotted cucumber, striped cucumber, whitefringed Bugs: harlequin, southern green stink, tarnished plant Caterpillars: cabbage looper, corn earworm, cutworms, imported cabbageworm, yellow woollybear Flies: cabbage maggot Leafminers Thrips Whiteflies		Noninsects: slugs, snails Thrips Weevils: cabbage curculio, vegetable	Crickets: northern mole Flies: cabbage maggot Noninsects: millipedes Thrips
Carrot	Beetles: carrot, flea, margined blister Caterpillars: parsleyworm, yellow woollybear Leafhoppers			Aphids Flies: carrot rust Thrips: onions

Carrot (CONT.)	Weevils: vegetable			Weevils: carrot, vegetable Wireworms
Cauliflower **See Cabbage**				
Celery	Aphids Beetles: carrot, flea Bugs: negro, tarnished plant Caterpillars: cabbage looper, obliquebanded leafroller, omnivorous leaftier Flies: cabbage maggot, carrot rust Leafhoppers: beet Noninsects: mites		Caterpillars Noninsects: mites Thrips Weevils: carrot	
Cherry	Aphids Beetles: Japanese Bugs: boxelder, harlequin, southern green stink Caterpillars: apple-and-thorn skeletonizer, eastern tent, eyespotted bud moth, fall cankerworm, fruittree leafroller, obliquebanded leafroller, omnivorous looper, redbanded leafroller, redhumped, western tent, western tussock moth, yellownecked, yellow woollybear Crickets: snowy tree Leafminers Noninsects: mites Scales Whiteflies	Aphids Caterpillars: codling moth, green fruitworm, oriental fruit moth Thrips Wasps: apple sawfly Weevils: apple curculio, plum curculio	Borers: California prionus, flatheaded appletree, lesser peachtree, shothole Leafhoppers: buffalo treehopper	
Citrus	Aphids Bugs: leaffooted, southern green stink, tarnished plant Caterpillars: cutworms, fruittree leafroller, omnivorous looper, puss, western tussock Leafhoppers Mealybugs: citrus Noninsects: mites	Aphids Bugs: harlequin, southern green stink Caterpillars: navel orangeworm, orangedog, orange tortrix Mealybugs	Borers: California prionus	Weevils

CROP	FOLIAGE	FLOWERS AND FRUITS	STEMS AND BRANCHES	ROOTS
Citrus (CONT.)	Scales Thrips Whiteflies			
Collard **See Cabbage**				
Corn	Aphids Beetles: bean leaf, carrot, cereal leaf, flea, green June, Japanese, spotted cucumber, striped blister, striped cucumber, whitefringed Bugs: chinch, harlequin, negro, southern green stink Caterpillars: cutworms, yellow woollybear Leafhoppers Thrips	Borers: European corn Caterpillars: corn earworm	Borers: lesser cornstalk, southern cornstalk, southwestern corn	Beetles: northern corn rootworm Wireworms
Cranberry	Caterpillars: gypsy moth, western tussock moth Leafhoppers Scales: oystershell Weevils	Caterpillars Weevils	Weevils	
Cucumber	Aphids Beetles: flea, spotted cucumber, striped cucumber Bugs: southern green stink, squash, tarnished plant Caterpillars: cutworms Leafhoppers: beet Noninsects: mites Thrips	Aphids Beetles: spotted cucumber, striped cucumber Bugs: squash, tarnished plant Caterpillars: pickleworm Thrips Whiteflies	Borers: squash vine Crickets: field	Weevils
Currant	Aphids Bugs: fourlined plant Caterpillars: fruittree leafroller, io moth, obliquebanded leafroller, whitelined sphinx moth, yellow woollybear Leafhoppers Mealybugs	Flies: currant fruit	Borers: flatheaded appletree	

Crop				
Currant (CONT.)	Noninsects: mites Scales: oystershell, walnut			
Eggplant	Aphids Beetles: Colorado potato, flea Bugs: harlequin, lace, southern green stink Caterpillars: cutworms, tomato hornworm Leafhoppers: potato Leafminers Noninsects: mites	Flies: pepper maggot	Borers: potato stalk, potato tuberworm	
Fig	Beetles: fig, green June Mealybugs Noninsects: mites Psyllids Scales	Beetles: green June Caterpillars: navel orangeworm Mealybugs		Wireworms
Garlic See Onion				
Gooseberry See Currant				
Grape	Aphids Beetles: flea, grape colaspis, spotted grapevine Bugs: boxelder, harlequin Caterpillars: corn earworm, grape berry moth, grapeleaf skeletonizer, omnivorous looper Crickets Leafhoppers Scales Thrips Whiteflies	Aphids Beetles: fig Thrips	Caterpillars: cutworms Crickets	Beetles: grape colaspis Borers: grape root Wireworms

CROP	FOLIAGE	FLOWERS AND FRUITS	STEMS AND BRANCHES	ROOTS
Lettuce	Aphids Beetles: flea Bugs: tarnished plant Caterpillars: cabbage looper, imported cabbageworm, omnivorous leafroller Noninsects: centipedes, mites		Weevils: vegetable Whiteflies	Aphids Noninsects: centipedes, millipedes
Mango	Leafhoppers: potato Mealybugs: citrus, longtailed, striped Noninsects: mites Thrips	Mealybugs: citrus, longtailed, striped Thrips	Mites	
Melon	Aphids Beetles: flea, grape colaspis, spotted cucumber, striped blister Bugs: squash Caterpillars: cabbage looper, yellow woollybear Leafhoppers: beet Noninsects: mites Whiteflies	Aphids Beetles: fig, spotted cucumber, squash, striped cucumber Bugs: squash Caterpillars: pickleworm	Borers: squash vine Thrips Whiteflies	Thrips
Okra	Aphids Beetles: flea, grape colaspis, striped cucumber Bugs: harlequin, southern green stink Caterpillars: corn earworm Whiteflies	Caterpillars: corn earworm	Whiteflies	
Onion	Beetles: margined blister, striped blister Leafminers		Caterpillars: cutworms Thrips Weevils: vegetable	Flies: onion maggot Thrips Wireworms
Orange See Citrus				

Plant			
Parsnip	Aphids		
Pea	Aphids Beetles: bean leaf, flea, spotted cucumber, striped blister, striped cucumber Bugs: Say stink Caterpillars: alfalfa, cabbage looper, green cloverworm, yellow woollybear Leafminers Whiteflies	Thrips Weevils: bean	Borers: lesser cornstalk
Peach	Aphids Beetles: Japanese Bugs: boxelder, southern green stink, tarnished plant Caterpillars: eastern tent, fall cankerworm, fall webworm, forest tent, obliquebanded leafroller, oriental fruit moth, spring cankerworm, walnut, yellownecked Mealybugs Scales	Beetles: fig, green June, Japanese Caterpillars: codling moth, oriental fruit moth Flies: walnut husk Mealybugs Scales Thrips	Borers: California prionus, flatheaded appletree, lesser peachtree, peachtree, roundheaded appletree, shothole Bugs: tarnished plant
Pear	Aphids Beetles: flea, green June Caterpillars: apple-and-thorn skeletonizer, codling moth, eastern tent, forest tent, fruittree leafroller, obliquebanded leafroller, yellownecked Scales Whiteflies	Beetles: fig, green June Bugs: apple red, tarnished plant Caterpillars: codling moth, green fruitworm Flies: apple maggot Scales Thrips Wasps: European apple sawfly	Borers: flatheaded appletree, roundheaded appletree, shothole, twig girdler
Pecan	Aphids Bugs: fourlined plant Caterpillars: fall webworm, omnivorous looper, walnut Leafhoppers: spittlebugs Noninsects: mites Scales	Bugs: fourlined plant, leaffooted, southern green stink Caterpillars: walnut Weevils: pecan	Borers: flatheaded appletree, shothole, twig girdler Scales

CROP	FOLIAGE	FLOWERS AND FRUITS	STEMS AND BRANCHES	ROOTS
Pepper	Aphids Beetles: Colorado potato, flea, striped blister Bugs: leaffooted, southern green stink Caterpillars: beet armyworm, corn earworm Leafhoppers: beet Leafminers Mealybugs Noninsects: mites Whiteflies	Flies: pepper maggot	Caterpillars: cutworms Whiteflies	
Plum	Aphids Beetles: flea, Japanese Caterpillars: eastern tent, fall cankerworm, orange tortrix, puss, redhumped, spring cankerworm, western tent, western tussock moth, whitelined sphinx moth, yellownecked Leafminers Mealybugs Noninsects: mites Scales	Beetles: green June Caterpillars: codling moth Flies: apple maggot, cherry fruit Mealybugs Scales Thrips Wasps: European apple sawfly Weevils: plum curculio	Borers: California prionus, flatheaded appletree, lesser peachtree, roundheaded appletree, shothole Crickets	
Potato	Aphids Beetles: carrot, Colorado potato, flea, margined blister, spotted cucumber, striped blister, striped cucumber, whitefringed Bugs: fourlined plant, harlequin, lace, leaffooted, Say stink Caterpillars: cabbage looper, cutworms, tomato hornworm Crickets: Jerusalem, northern mole Leafhoppers: beet, potato Leafminers Mealybugs Whiteflies		Beetles: flea Borers: European corn, potato stalk, potato tuberworm Weevils: vegetable	Borers: potato tuberworm Noninsects: millipedes Wireworms
Pumpkin *See Squash*				

224

Crop				
Quince **See Apple**				
Radish	Aphids Beetles: black blister, flea, striped blister Bugs: harlequin Caterpillars: cabbage looper, imported cabbageworm, yellow woollybear Leafminers			Aphids Flies: cabbage maggot Weevils: cabbage curculio, vegetable Wireworms
Raspberry	Aphids Bugs: negro Caterpillars: fruittree leafroller, green cloverworm, orange tortrix, strawberry crown moth Noninsects: mites Scales Whiteflies		Borers: flatheaded appletree, raspberry cane	
Spinach	Aphids Beetles: flea, margined blister Caterpillars: cabbage looper, cutworms Leafhoppers: beet Leafminers Weevils: vegetable			
Squash	Aphids Beetles: spotted cucumber, striped cucumber, squash Bugs: squash Caterpillars: corn earworm, yellow woollybear Leafhoppers: beet Whiteflies	Borers: squash vine Caterpillars: pickleworm	Borers: squash vine Thrips	Aphids
Strawberry	Aphids Beetles: grape colaspis, whitefringed Bugs: leaffooted, negro, tarnished plant	Mealybugs Noninsects: mites, pill bugs, slugs	Borers: strawberry crown	Noninsects: millipedes, pill bugs

CROP	FOLIAGE	FLOWERS AND FRUITS	STEMS AND BRANCHES	ROOTS
Strawberry (CONT.)	Caterpillars: cutworms, green cloverworm, obliquebanded leafroller, omnivorous leaftier, strawberry crown moth Mealybugs Noninsects: mites Scales Thrips			
Tomato	Aphids Beetles: black blister, Colorado potato, flea, margined blister, spotted cucumber, striped blister Bugs: green stink, lace, leaffooted Caterpillars: cabbage looper, corn earworm, cutworms, tomato hornworm, whitelined sphinx moth Leafhoppers: beet, potato Leafminers	Beetles: fig, spotted cucumber Caterpillars: corn earworm, tomato hornworm, whitelined sphinx moth Flies: pepper maggot Thrips Weevils	Borers: potato stalk, potato tuberworm Caterpillars: cutworms Crickets	
Turnip	Aphids Beetles: flea, striped blister, whitefringed Bugs: harlequin, tarnished plant Caterpillars: cabbage looper, cutworms, imported cabbageworm Leafminers		Aphids Borers: lesser cornstalk Thrips Weevils: cabbage curculio, vegetable	Borers: lesser cornstalk Flies: cabbage maggot Noninsects: millipedes, slugs, sow bugs Thrips
Walnut	Aphids Bugs: lace Caterpillars: fall webworm, fruittree leafroller, hickory tussock moth, omnivorous looper, redhumped, walnut, western tussock moth Mealybugs Scales	Aphids Caterpillars: codling moth, navel orangeworm, orange tortrix Flies: walnut husk Mealybugs Scales	Aphids Borers: California prionus	

FOR FURTHER READING

Borror, D. J. and De Long, D. M. *Introduction to the Study of Insects.* 3rd ed. New York: Holt, Rinehart & Winston, 1970.

Dalton, S. *Borne on the Wind: The Extraordinary World of Insects in Flight.* New York: Reader's Digest Press, 1975.

DeBach, P. *Biological Control of Insect Pests and Weeds.* New York: Reinhold, 1964.

Fabre, J. H. *Social Life in the Insect World.* Detroit: Gale Research, 1974.

Forbes, A. W. *Our Garden Friends the Bugs.* New York: Exposition Press, 1962.

Goldstein, J., ed. *The Least Is Best Pesticide Strategy.* Emmaus, Pa.: JG Press, 1978.

Parenti, U. *Insects: World of Miniature Beauty.* New York: New Dimensions Library, 1972.

Swan, L. and Papp, C. S. *The Common Insects of North America.* New York: Harper & Row, 1972.

Teale, E. W. *The Strange Lives of Familiar Insects.* New York: Dodd, Mead & Co., 1962.

Yepsen, R. B., ed. *Organic Plant Protection.* Emmaus, Pa.: Rodale Press, 1976.

PHOTOGRAPH
CREDITS

Without the stunning slides contributed by the following photographers, this book could not have been possible: Animal and Plant Health Inspection Service (APHIS), USDA; Max E. Badgley; Glenn L. Berkey and Roy W. Rings, Ohio Agricultural Research and Development Center; Clemson State University Extension Service; Robert P. Carr; James A. Cunningham and Jerome Wexler, Visual Teaching, Inc.; Robert Gossington; Grant Heilman Photography; Thomas A. Henley; Lee Jenkins; Ray R. Kriner; Dwight R. Kuhn; Gerard Lemmo; Sturgis McKeever; Karl Maslowski; Ann Moreton; Oregon State University Extension Service; James E. Roberts; Edward S. Ross; Donald L. Schuder; Patricia Seip, Rodale Press Photography Department.

INDEX

Abdomen, of insect, 1
spiracles in, 3
Acalymma vittata, 56
Acanthoscelides obtectus, 197
Achyra rantalis, 112
Acrididae, 149
Acyrthosiphon pisum, 12
Adult
eyes of, 6
as stage of metamorphosis, 3
Agriculture, control of insects
for, ix, 6–8
Almonds
borers in, 72
caterpillars on, 119, 124
scale on, 189
Alsophila pometaria, 108
Altica chalybea, 34
Amphipyra pyramidoides, 127
Amyelois transitella, 119
Anasa tristis, 90
Antennae, of insect
development of, during
metamorphosis, 3
location of, 1
sensory organs on, 5
Anthophila pariana, 95
Antlion, 170
Ants, 15–16, 17
aphids and, 9
control for, 8
Aonidiella aurantii, 188
Aphelinus mali, as predator
of aphids, 13
Aphids, 9–13
bean, 10
controls for, 7, 8, 9
green peach, 11
incomplete metamorphosis of, 3
pea, 12
reproduction cycle of, 9
spinach, 11
woolly apple, 13
Aphis fabae, 10
Apis mellifera, 19
Apple-and-thorn skeletonizer, 95
Apple curculio, 196
Apple maggot, 157
Apple red bug, 76

Apples
aphids on, 13
beetles on, 33, 34, 37
borers in, 62, 71, 72
bugs on, 76
caterpillars on, 95–137 passim
cicadas on, 142
crickets on, 148
flies and maggots on, 156
mealybugs on, 183
sawflies on, 20
scale on, 189, 191
weevils on, 196, 201
Apricots
borers in, 62, 64, 66, 72
caterpillars on, 120, 123, 124, 129,
135, 137
scale on, 189
Arachnida class, 212
Archips argyrospilus, 111
Argyrotaenia citrana, 123
Argyrotaenia velutinana, 128
Army cutworm, 96
Arthropoda, as phylum
within Animal Kingdom, 1
Artichoke, caterpillars on, 97
Artichoke plume moth, 97
Asilidae, 166
Asparagus
beetles on, 27
bugs on, 88
caterpillars on, 130, 138
centipedes on, 210
Asparagus beetle, 2, 27, 52
Asparagus fern caterpillar, 98
Assassin bug, 77
as predator of beetles, 46
Automeris io, 118
Avocado, mealybugs on, 182, 184

Bacillus popullae, 8. See also
Milky spore disease
Bacillus thuringiensis, 8
Bacteria, to control insects, 8
Bananas, mealybugs on, 184
Barriers, to control insects, 7
Beak. *See* Mouthparts
Bean aphid, 10
Bean leaf beetle, 28

Beans
   aphids on, 10, 12
   beetles on, 28, 33, 46, 55, 56
   borers in, 65
   bugs on, 85, 88, 89
   caterpillars on, 99–138 passim
   crickets on, 145
   flies and maggots on, 162
   leafhoppers on, 176
   millipedes on, 211
   weevils on, 197
   wireworms on, 208
Bean weevil, 197
Bees, 15–16
   bumble, 18
   complete metamorphosis of, 3
   honey, 19
Beet armyworm, 98
Beet leafhopper, 174
Beetles, 25–26
   asparagus, 2, 27
   bean leaf, 28
   carrot, 29
   clover rootworm, 33
   Colorado potato, 30
   complete metamorphosis of, 3
   controls for, 7, 8, 25–26
   daw bug, 38
   downy leather-wing, 50
   as example of insect order, 1–2
   fiery searcher, 35
   fig, 31
   flea, 32
   grape colaspis, 33
   grape flea, 34
   ground, 35, 36
      as predator, 30, 105, 113
   Japanese, 37
   June, 38
   lady, 39–43
      as predator, 9, 27, 189, 212
   margined blister, 44
   May, 38
   mealybug destroyer, 45
      as predator, 182
   Mexican bean, 46
   northern corn rootworm, 47
   Pennsylvania leather-wing, 51
   rove, 48
      as predator, 157
   sap, 49
   soldier, 50, 51
   spotted asparagus, 52
   spotted cucumber, 53
      spotted grapevine, 54
      striped blister, 55
      striped cucumber, 56
      tiger, 57
      whitefringed, 58
Beets
   aphids on, 10
   beetles on, 29, 55
   caterpillars on, 98, 107, 112,
      130, 136, 138
   leafhoppers on, 174
   weevils on, 203
   wireworms on, 208
Berries. See also Blackberries;
   Blueberries; Boysenberries;
   Gooseberries; Raspberries;
   Strawberries
   beetles on, 31
Bigeyed bug, 78
   as predator of leafhopper, 174
Blackberries. See also Berries
   borers in, 70
   bugs on, 80, 87
   caterpillars on, 118, 120, 129,
      132, 137
   crickets on, 148
   flies and maggots on, 162
Black swallowtail butterfly, 125
Blissus leucopterus, 81
Blood, of insect, 3
Blueberries
   beetles on, 34, 87, 137
   flies and maggots on, 156
   weevils on, 201
Blue sharpshooter, 175
Body, segments of, 1
Bombus sp., 18
Borers, 59–60. See also Caterpillars
   European corn, 61
   flatheaded appletree, 62
   fruittree bark, 72
   grape root, 63
   lesser peachtree, 64
   limabean pod, 65
   peachtree, 66
   pickleworm, 67
   plumtree, 64
   potato stalk, 68
   potato tuberworm, 69
   raspberry crown, 70
   roundheaded appletree, 71
   shothole, 72

southwestern corn, 73
squash vine, 74
wood, 2
Bothynus gibbosus, 29
Boxelder bug, 79
Boxelder tree, bugs on, 79
Boysenberries. *See also* Berries
borers in, 70
Braconidae, 22
Braconid wasp, 22
as parasite of insects, 16
as predator of borers, 61
as predator of caterpillars,
100, 124, 133
Breathing, of insect, 3
Broadwinged katydid, 150
Broccoli
beetles on, 32
caterpillars on, 99, 104
flies and maggots on, 157
weevils on, 198
Brown stink bug, 80
Brussels sprouts
bugs on, 84
flies and maggots on, 157
Budworm, 107
Buffalo treehopper, 179
Bugs, 75
apple red, 76
assassin, 77
as predator, 46
bigeyed, 78
as predator, 174
boxelder, 79
brown stink, 80
calico, 84
chinch, 81
controls for, 7, 8
eggplant lace, 82
fourlined plant, 83
harlequin, 84
incomplete metamorphosis of, 3, 75
insidious flower, 86
leaffooted, 85
minute pirate, 86
negro, 87
Say stink, 88
southern green stink, 89
squash, 90
tarnished plant, 91
Bumble bee, 18
Buprestidae, 2

Butterflies. *See also* Caterpillars
complete metamorphosis of, 3

Cabbage
beetles on, 32
bugs on, 80
caterpillars on, 99, 104, 107,
117, 130, 138
flies and maggots on, 157, 162
millipedes on, 211
weevils on, 198, 203
Cabbage curculio, 198
Cabbage looper, 99
Cabbage maggot, 157
Calico bug, 84
California red scale, 188
Calosoma scrutator, 35
Cankerworm. *See* Fall cankerworm;
Spring cankerworm
Carabus nemoralis, 36
Carpocapsa pomonella, 100
Carrot beetle, 29
Carrot rust fly, 158
Carrots
beetles on, 29
caterpillars on, 125, 130, 138
flies and maggots on, 158
millipedes on, 211
weevils on, 199, 203
wireworms on, 208
Carrot weevil, 199
Caterpillars, 93–94. *See also* Borers
apple-and-thorn skeletonizer, 95
army cutworm, 96
artichoke plume moth, 97
asparagus fern, 98
beet armyworm, 98
black swallowtail butterfly, 125
budworm, 107
cabbage looper, 99
celeryworm, 125
codling moth, 100
controls for, 7, 8, 94
corn earworm, 101
cotton square borer, 102
cutworms, 103
diamondback moth, 104
eastern tent, 105
eyespotted bud moth, 106
fall armyworm, 107
fall cankerworm, 108

Caterpillars *(continued)*
    fall webworm, 109
    forest tent, 110
    fruittree leafroller, 111
    garden webworm, 112
    giant swallowtail, 122
    grape berry moth, 113
    grapeleaf skeletonizer, 114
    gray hairstreak, 102
    green fruitworm, 115
    gypsy moth, 116
    imported cabbageworm, 117
    io moth, 118
    legs of, 1
    navel orangeworm, 119
    obliquebanded leafroller, 120
    omnivorous leaftier, 121
    orangedog, 122
    orange tortrix, 123
    Oriental fruit moth, 124
    parsleyworm, 125
    puss, 126
    pyramidal fruitworm, 127
    redbanded leafroller, 128
    redhumped, 129
    redhumped appleworm, 129
    rose leaftier, 120
    saltmarsh, 130
    spring cankerworm, 131
    strawberry crown moth, 132
    strawberry fruitworm, 121
    tomato hornworm, 133
    walnut, 134
    western tussock moth, 135
    whitelined sphinx moth, 136
    yellownecked, 137
    yellow woollybear, 138
    zebra, 139
Cauliflower
    beetles on, 32
    bugs on, 84
    caterpillars on, 99, 104, 117, 138
    flies and maggots on, 157
    weevils on, 198
Cedar chips, to control insects, 7
Celery
    bugs on, 87
    caterpillars on, 99, 120, 125,
        130, 138
    flies and maggots on, 158
    leafhoppers on, 176
    weevils on, 199
Celeryworm, 125
Centipede, 209, 210

Ceramica picta, 139
Ceratitis capitata, 163
Cercopidae, 178
Cerotoma trifurcata, 28
Ceutorhynchus rapae, 198
Chalcid wasp, as predator
    of aphids, 13, 16
    of beetles, 27, 52
    of psyllids, 186
    of scale, 188
Chard, aphids on, 10
Chauliognathus pennsylvanicus, 51
Cherries
    beetles on, 37
    borers in, 62, 64, 66, 72
    bugs on, 84
    caterpillars on, 106–38 passim
    crickets on, 148
    flies and maggots on, 156, 159
    scale on, 191
    walkingsticks on, 152
    weevils on, 201
Cherry fruit fly, 159
Cherry maggot, 159
Chilopoda class, 210
Chinch bug, 81
Chlorochroa sayi, 88
Choristoneura rosaceana, 120
Chrysalis, during pupation, 93–94
Chrysobothris femorata, 62
Chrysopa sp., 171
Cicadas, 141
    periodical, 142
Circulation, of insects, 3
Circulifer tenellus, 174
Citrus mealybug, 182
Citrus thrips, 194
Classification. *See* Scientific
    classification of insects
Clover rootworm beetle, 33
Cnephasia longana, 121
Cocoon, as protection for pupa, 3, 93
Codling moth, 100
Colaspis brunnea, 33
Coleoptera order, 1
    beetles, 24–58
    borers, 59–74
    weevils, 195–203
    wireworms, 207–8
Collards, bugs on, 84

Collars, to protect young plants, 7
Colorado potato beetle, 30
Companion planting, to control insects, 6
Comstock mealybug, 183
Conotrachelus nenuphar, 201
Controlling insects. *See* Insects, control of
Corimelaena pulicaria, 87
Corn
    beetles on, 29, 31, 33, 47,
        53, 55, 58
    borers in, 61, 73
    bugs on, 80, 81
    caterpillars on, 98, 101, 107,
        112, 118, 130, 138
    millipedes on, 211
    spittlebugs on, 178
    wireworms on, 208
Corn earworm, 101
Cotinis texana, 31
Cotton square borer, 102
Cottonycushion scale, 189
Creosote, to control bugs, 81
Crickets, 143–44
    field, 145
    incomplete metamorphosis of, 3
    Jerusalem, 146
    northern mole, 147
    snowy tree, 148
Crioceris asparagi, 27
Crioceris duodecimpunctata, 52
Crop rotation, to control insects, 6–7
Cryptolaemus montrouzieri, 45
Cucumbers
    beetles on, 53, 56
    borers in, 67, 74
    bugs on, 80
    caterpillars on, 107
    centipedes on, 210
    crickets on, 145
Cultivation, to control insects, 6
Curculio. *See* Apple curculio;
    Cabbage curculio; Plum curculio;
    Rhubarb curculio
Curculio caryae, 200
Currant fruit fly, 160
Currants
    borers in, 62
    bugs on, 83
    caterpillars on, 118, 120, 136
    flies and maggots on, 160

Cutworm, 7, 103. *See also* Army cutworm
Cycloneda sp., 39

Datana integerrima, 134
Datana ministra, 137
Dates, thrips on, 194
Daw bug, 38
Dehydration, caused by
    diatomaceous earth, 8
Dermaptera order, 153
Diabrotica longicornis, 47
Diabrotica undecimpunctata howardi, 53
Diacrisia virginica, 138
Diamondback moth, 104
Diaphania nitidalis, 67
Diapheromera femorata, 152
Diatomaceous earth, 8
Diatraea grandiosella, 73
Digestive system, of insects, 5
Dill, weevils on, 199
Diplopoda class, 211
Diptera order, 155
    flies, 156–68
Doodlebug, 170
Doom. *See Bacillus popullae;*
    Milky spore disease
Dormant-oil spray, 7
Downy leather-wing, 50
Dusting, to control insects, 8

Earwigs, 153
    European, 154
    incomplete metamorphosis of, 3
Earworm. *See* Corn earworm
Eastern field wireworm, 208
Eastern tent caterpillar, 105
Eating habits, of insects, 3, 5
Ecosystem, insect role in, ix
Egg, as stage of metamorphosis, 3
Eggplant
    beetles on, 30, 53
    borers in, 68, 69
    bugs on, 82
    caterpillars on, 133, 138
    flies and maggots on, 165
    leafhoppers on, 176
Eggplant lace bug, 82

Elytra, of beetles, 25
Empoasca fabae, 176
Endopiza viteana, 113
Epicauta pestifera, 44
Epicauta vittata, 55
Epilachna varivestis, 46
Epochra canadensis, 160
Eriosoma lanigerum, 13
Estigmene acrea, 130
Etiella zinckenella, 65
European apple sawfly, 20
European corn borer, 61
European earwig, 154
Euschistus servus, 80
Euxoa auxiliaris, 96
Exoskeleton, 1
    molting of, 2-3
Eyes
    compound and single, 5-6
    location of, 1
Eyespotted bud moth, 106

Fall armyworm, 107
Fall cankerworm, 108
Fall webworm, 109
False hellebore. *See* Hellebore
False legs. *See* Prolegs
Farming, control of insects for, ix
Feeding. *See* Eating habits, of insects
Feel, sense of, in insects, 5
Fels-Naphtha, added to water spray, 7
Field cricket, 145
Fiery searcher beetle, 35
Fig beetle, 31
Figs
    caterpillars on, 119
    scale on, 188, 189
Flatheaded appletree borer, 62
Flea beetle, 32
Flies, 155. *See also* Maggots
    apple maggot, 156
    cabbage maggot, 157
    carrot rust, 158
    cherry fruit, 159
    complete metamorphosis of, 3
    controlled by Stikem
        and Tanglefoot, 7
    currant fruit, 160

flower, 161
hover, 161
leafminers, 162
Mediterranean fruit, 163
onion maggot, 164
pepper maggot, 165
robber, 166
syrphid, 9
tachinid, 167
    as predator, 37, 53, 61,
        90, 101, 154
walnut husk, 168
Flour, to control insects, 7
Flower flies, 161
Food chain, insect role in, ix
Forest tent caterpillar, 110
Forficula auricularia, 154
Formicidae, 17
Fourlined plant bug, 83
Froghoppers, 178
Fruit flies. *See also* Flies
    controlled by netting, 7
Fruittree bark borer, 72
Fruittree leafroller, 111
Fruitworms. *See* Caterpillars

Garden centipede, 210
Gardening, control of
    insects for, ix, 6-8
Garden maintenance, 6
Garden symphylan, 210
Garden webworm, 112
Gargaphia solani, 82
Garlic, to control insects, 7
Geocoris pallens, 78
Giant swallowtail, 122
Gooseberries. *See also* Berries
    bugs on, 83
    flies and maggots on, 160
Gourd, borers in, 74
Grape berry moth, 113
Grape colaspis beetle, 33
Grape flea beetle, 34
Grapeleaf skeletonizer, 114
Grape root borer, 63
Grapes
    beetles on, 33, 34, 37, 54
    borers in, 63
    caterpillars on, 113, 114, 136, 138

leafhoppers on, 175
mealybugs on, 183
scale on, 188, 189
thrips on, 194
Graphocephala coccinea, 177
Graphognathus leucoloma, 58
Grapholitha molesta, 124
Grasshoppers, 143–44, 149
   control for, 8
   incomplete metamorphosis of, 3
Gray hairstreak, 102
Green fruitworm, 115
Greenhouse whitefly, 206
Green lacewing, 171
Green peach aphid, 11
Ground beetle, 35, 36
   as predator of caterpillars, 105,
      113
   as predator of Colorado
      potato beetle, 30
Ground-cherry, borers in, 68
Grubs, 25. *See also* Borers
   controls for 7, 8, 26, 37, 38
Gryllus sp., 145
Gypsy moth, 116

Hairs, sensory, 5
Harlequin bug, 84
Harrisina sp., 114
Head, of insects, 1
Hearing, sense of, 5
Heart, of insects, 3
Heliothis zea, 101
Hellebore, 8
Hemiptera order, 1
   bugs, 75–91
Herbs, to control insects, 7
Hesperoleon abdominalis, 170
Hexapoda, as class
   within Animal Kingdom, 1
Hippodamia convergens, 40
Homoptera order
   aphids, 9–13
   cicadas, 14
   leafhoppers, 173–77
   mealybugs, 181–84
   psyllids, 185–86
   scales, 187–91
   spittlebugs, 178

treehoppers, 179
whiteflies, 205–6
Honey bee, 19
Hoplocampa brevis, 21
Hoplocampa testudinea, 20
Hornworm. *See* Tomato hornworm
Horseradish, bugs on, 84
Hover flies, 161
Hylemya antiqua, 164
Hylemya brassicae, 157
Hyles lineata, 136
Hymenoptera order, 15–16
   ants, 17
   bees, 18–19
   sawflies, 20–21
   wasps, 22–23
Hyphantria cunea, 109

Icerya purchasi, 189
Ichneumon wasp, as parasite
   and predator, 15, 16
Imported cabbageworm, 117
Insecta, as class within
   Animal Kingdom, 1
Insecticides, ix, 7–8
Insects
   bodily functions of, 3, 5
   control of, ix, 6–8
   diagram of, xii
   growth of, 2–3
   importance of, to ecosystem, ix
   physical characteristics of, 1
   sensory organs of, 5–6
Insidious flower bug, 86
Instar, 2–3
Interplanting, to control insects, 6
Io moth, 118

Japanese beetle, 37
Jaws. *See* Mouthparts
Jerusalem cricket, 146
June beetle, 38

Kale, caterpillars on, 99, 117
Katydids, 143–44, 150
Kohlrabi
   bugs on, 84
   caterpillars on, 104, 117

Lacewings, 169
  antlion, 170
  complete metamorphosis of, 3
  doodlebug, 170
  groon, 171
  as predator, 9, 169–71, 212
Lady beetle, 39–43
  as predator, 9, 27, 189, 212
Larva
  eyes of, 6
  as stage of complete metamorphosis, 3
Leaffooted bug, 85
Leafhoppers, 173
  beet, 174
  blue sharpshooter, 175
  controls for, 7
  potato, 176
  redbanded, 177
Leafminers, 162
  controls for, 7
Leafroller. See Fruittree leafroller;
  Obliquebanded leafroller;
  Redbanded leafroller
Leather-wing
  downy, 50
  Pennsylvania, 51
Legs, of insects, 1. See also Prolegs
Lepidoptera order
  borers, 59–74
  caterpillars, 93–139
Lepidosaphes beckii, 190
Leptinotarsa decemlineata, 30
Leptocoris trivittatus, 79
Leptoglossus phyllopus, 85
Lesser peachtree borer, 64
Lettuce
  caterpillars on, 99, 130
  centipedes on, 210
  flies and maggots on, 162
  weevils on, 203
  wireworms on, 208
Limabean pod borer, 65
Limonius agonus, 208
Liriomyza sp., 162
Listroderes costirostris obliquus, 203
Listronotus oregonensis, 199
Lithophane antennata, 115
Lixus concavus, 202
Locusts, 149
Longtailed mealybug, 184
Lygidea mendax, 76

Lygus lineolaris, 91
Lymantria dispar, 116

Maggots, 155. See also Flies
  control for, 8
Magicicada septendecim, 142
Malacosoma americanum, 105
Malacosoma disstria, 110
Manduca quinquemaculata, 133
Mantidae, 151
Mantids, 143–44, 151
  incomplete metamorphosis of, 3
Margined blister beetle, 44
May beetle, 38
Mealybug destroyer beetle, 45
  as predator, 182
Mealybugs, 181
  citrus, 182
  comstock, 183
  longtailed, 184
Mediterranean fruit fly, 163
Megalopyge opercularis, 126
Melittia satyriniformis, 74
Melons
  beetles on, 33, 53, 55, 56
  borers in, 67, 74
  bugs on, 90
  caterpillars on, 136, 138
  crickets on, 149
Metamorphosis, complete
  and incomplete, 3
Mexican bean beetle, 46
  controls for, 7
Microcentrum rhombifolium, 150
Milky spore disease,
  to control beetle grubs, 37, 38
Millipedes, 209, 211
Mint, bugs on, 83
Minute pirate bug, 86
Mites, 209, 212
  controls for, 7, 8
Mollusca phylum, 213
Molting
  exoskeleton and, 1
  process of, 2–3
Moths. See also Caterpillars
  complete metamorphosis of, 3
  controlled by Stikem
    and Tanglefoot, 7

Mouthparts
  basic types of, 3
  location of, 1
Mud dauber wasp, as predator, 16
Mulch, to control insects, 6
Murgantia histrionica, 84
Mustard
  bugs on, 84
  caterpillars on, 117
Myzus persicae, 11

Navel orangeworm, 119
Nectar, as food, 5
Negro bug, 87
Neocurtilla hexadactyla, 147
Neokolla circellata, 175
Netting, to control insects, 7
Neuroptera order, 169
  lacewings, 170-71
Nezara viridula, 89
Nitidula sp., 49
Noctuidae, 103
Northern corn rootworm, 47
Northern mole cricket, 147
Nymph
  eyes of, 6
  as stage of incomplete
    metamorphosis, 3

Obliquebanded leafroller, 120
Ocelli, 6
Odor, used by insects, 5
Oecanthus fultoni, 148
Olla abdominalis, 41
Omnivorous leaftier, 121
Onion maggot, 164
Onions
  caterpillars on, 130
  weevils on, 203
  wireworms on, 208
Orangedog caterpillar, 122
Oranges
  bugs on, 84, 85
  caterpillars on, 102, 119, 122, 123
  leafhoppers on, 176
  mealybugs on, 182, 184
  scale on, 188, 189, 190
  thrips on, 194

Orange tortrix, 123
Orgyia vetusta, 135
Oriental fruit moth, 124
Orius sp., 86
Orthoptera order, 143-44
  crickets, 145-48
  grasshoppers, 149
  katydids, 150
  mantids, 151
  walkingsticks, 152
Ostrinia nubilalis, 61

Paleacrita vernata, 131
Papilio cresphontes, 122
Papilio polyxenes asterius, 125
Parsley
  beetles on, 29
  caterpillars on, 99, 125
  flies and maggots on, 158
  weevils on, 199
Parsleyworm, 125
Parsnips
  beetles on, 29
  caterpillars on, 125
  flies and maggots on, 158
Parthenogenesis, 15
Pea aphid, 12
Peaches
  beetles on, 37
  borers in, 62, 64, 66, 71, 72
  bugs on, 80, 85, 89
  caterpillars on, 109-37 passim
  crickets on, 148
  flies and maggots on, 168
  mealybugs on, 183
  scale on, 189, 191
  thrips on, 194
  weevils on, 201
Peachtree borer, 66
  lesser, 64
Peanuts, beetles on, 58
Pear psylla, 186
Pears
  aphids on, 13
  borers in, 62, 72
  caterpillars on, 100-137 passim
  flies and maggots on, 159
  mealybugs on, 183
  psyllids on, 186
  sawflies on, 21

Pears *(continued)*
  scale on, 191
  weevils on, 196, 201
Pear sawfly, 21
Peas
  aphids on, 10, 12
  beetles on, 28, 53, 55, 56
  borers in, 65
  bugs on, 85, 88
  caterpillars on, 98, 99, 101,
    112, 121, 138
  weevils on, 197
  wireworms on, 208
Pecans
  borers in, 62
  bugs on, 89
  caterpillars on, 109, 134, 137
  scale on, 189, 191
  weevils on, 200
Pecan weevil, 200
Pelidnota punctata, 54
Pennisetia marginata, 70
Pennsylvania leather-wing, 51
Pepper maggot, 165
Peppers
  beetles on, 30
  caterpillars on, 98, 101, 133
  flies and maggots on, 162, 165
  scale on, 189
Periodical cicada, 142
Perma-Guard. *See* Diatomaceous earth
Pesticides. *See* Insecticides; Sprays
Pests, insects as, ix, 6
Phthorimaea operculella, 69
Phyllophaga sp., 38
Phyllotreta striolata, 32
Picking insects by hand, 7
Pickleworm borer, 67
Pieris rapae, 117
Planococcus citri, 182
Planting times, to control insects, 7
Platyptilia carduidactyla, 97
Plowing, to control insects, 6
Plum curculio, 201
Plums
  beetles on, 34, 37
  borers in, 62, 66, 71, 72
  caterpillars, 106–37 passim
  crickets on, 148
  flies and maggots on, 156, 159
  mealybugs on, 184

weevils on, 201
Plumtree borer, 64
Plutella xylostella, 104
Podabrus tomentosus, 50
Poecilocapsus lineatus, 83
Pollinators
  bees as, 15–16, 17, 18
  wasps as, 15–16, 22, 23
Popillia japonica, 37
Potatoes
  beetles on, 29, 30, 33, 38,
    53, 55, 58
  borers in, 68
  bugs on, 82, 85, 88, 89
  caterpillars on, 99, 101, 107, 133
  crickets on, 146
  flies and maggots on, 162
  leafhoppers on, 174, 176
  mealybugs on, 182
  millipedes on, 211
  scale on, 189
  treehoppers on, 179
  weevils on, 203
  wireworms on, 208
Potato leafhopper, 176
Potato stalk borer, 68
Potato tuberworm, 69
Praying mantids, 151
Proboscis, for sucking nectar, 5
Prolegs
  on caterpillars and sawflies, 1, 93
  loss of, during pupal stage, 3
Pseudococcus adonidum, 184
Pseudococcus comstocki, 183
Psila rosae, 158
Psylla pyricola, 186
Psyllids, 185–86
Pumpkin
  beetles on, 56
  borers in, 67, 74
  bugs on, 90
Pupa, as stage of complete
  metamorphosis, 3, 93–94
Purple scale, 190
Puss caterpillar, 126
Pyramidal fruitworm, 127
Pyrethrum, ix, 8

Quadraspidiotus perniciosus, 191
Queen ants, 15

238

Queen bees and wasps, 15–16
Quince
    aphids on, 13
    beetles on, 37
    borers in, 71, 72
    caterpillars on, 95, 100, 110,
        115, 135, 137
    psyllids on, 186
    sawflies on, 21
    scale on, 189, 191
    weevils on, 196, 201

Radishes
    bugs on, 84
    caterpillars on, 99, 117
    centipedes on, 210
    flies and maggots on, 157
    weevils on, 203
Raspberries. *See also* Berries
    beetles on, 37
    borers in, 62, 70
    bugs on, 87
    caterpillars on, 120, 132
Raspberry crown borer, 70
Redbanded leafhopper, 177
Redbanded leafroller, 128
Redhumped appleworm, 129
Redhumped caterpillar, 129
Reduviidae, 77
Reproduction, during adult stage, 3
Resistant varieties, to control
    insects, 7
Respiration, of insects, 3
Rhagoletis cingulata, 159
Rhagoletis completa, 168
Rhagoletis pomonella, 156
Rhubarb
    aphids on, 10
    beetles on, 37
    leafhoppers on, 176
    weevils on, 202
Rhubarb curculio, 202
Robber flies, 166
Rodolia cardinalis, 43
Rootworm
    clover, 33
    northern corn, 47
Rose leaftier, 120
Rotenone, ix, 8
Roundheaded appletree borer, 71

Rove beetle, 48
    as predator, 157
Ryania, to control insects, 8

Sabadilla dust, to control insects, 8
Saltmarsh caterpillar, 130
Sanitation, in garden, 6
San Jose scale, 191
Sap beetle, 49
Saperda candida, 71
Sawflies, 15–16
    control of, 8
    European apple, 20
    legs of, 1
    pear, 21
Say stink bug, 88
Scale, 187
    California red, 188
    cottonycushion, 189
    incomplete metamorphosis of, 3
    lack of mouth in adult male, 3
    purple, 190
    San Jose, 191
Scent, used by insects, 5
Schizura concinna, 129
Scientific classification
    of insects, 1–2
Scirtothrips citri, 194
Scolytus rugulosus, 72
Scutellum, of true bugs, 75
Sensory organs, of insects, 5
Shothole borer, 72
Sight, of insects, 5–6
Skeleton. *See* Exoskeleton
Slugs, 209, 213
    control of, 8
Smell, sense of, 5
Snails, 209, 213
Snowy tree cricket, 148
Soapy water spray, 7
Soldier beetle, 50, 51
Southern green stink bug, 89
Southwestern corn borer, 73
Soybeans, beetles on, 28
Spider mite, 212
Spider mite destroyer, 42
Spilonota ocellana, 106

Spinach
  aphids on, 10
  caterpillars on, 98, 99, 107
  flies and maggots on, 162
  weevils on, 203
Spinach aphid, 11
Spiracles, 3
Spittlebugs, 178
Spodoptera exigua, 98
Spodoptera frugiperda, 107
Spotted asparagus beetle, 27, 52
Spotted cucumber beetle, 53
Spotted grapevine beetle, 54
Sprays, to control insects, 7–8
Spring cankerworm, 131
Squash
  beetles on, 53, 56
  borers in, 67, 74
  bugs on, 90
  caterpillars on, 101, 138
  crickets on, 148
Squash bug, 90
  control of, 7
Squash vine borer, 74
Staphylinidae, 48
Stenopelmatus fuscus, 146
Stethorus picipes, 42
Stictocephala bubalus, 179
Stikem, to control moths and flies, 7, 64
Stink bug. *See* Brown stink bug;
  Say stink bug; Southern
  green stink bug

Strawberries. *See also* Berries
  beetles on, 33, 34, 38
  caterpillars on, 112, 120, 121, 132
  millipedes on, 211
Strawberry crown moth, 132
Strawberry fruitworm, 121
Striped blister beetle, 55
Striped cucumber beetle, 56
Strymon melinus, 102
Sweet gum, caterpillars on, 129
Sweet potatoes, caterpillars on, 107
Symphylan, garden, 210
Synanthedon bibionipennis, 132
Synanthedon exitiosa, 66
Synanthedon pictipes, 64
Syrphidae, 161
Syrphid fly, as predator, 9

Tachinidae, 167
Tachinid fly, 167
  as predator
    of beetles, 37, 53
    of borers, 61
    of bugs, 90
    of caterpillars, 101
    of earwigs, 154
Tachypterellus quadrigibbus, 196
Tanglefoot, to control insects, 7
Tarnished plant bug, 91
Taste, sense of, 5
Tetracha virginica, 57
Thorax, 1
  spiracles in, 3
Thrips, 193–94
  control of, 8
  incomplete metamorphosis of, 3
Thysanoptera order, 193–94
Tiger beetle, 57
Tiphia wasp, as predator, 37
Tomatoes
  beetles on, 30, 53, 55
  borers in, 68, 69
  bugs on, 80, 82, 85, 89
  caterpillars on, 98, 99, 101, 107,
    133, 136
  centipedes on, 210
  crickets on, 145
  flies and maggots on, 165
  leafhoppers on, 174
  millipedes on, 211
  treehoppers on, 179
  weevils on, 203
Tomato hornworm, 133
Touch, sense of, 5
Transplants, protected by collars, 7
Treehopper, buffalo, 179
Tree sap, beetles feeding on, 49
Trialeurodes vaporariorum, 206
Trichobaris trinotata, 68
Trichogramma wasp, as predator
  of caterpillars, 98–138 passim
Trichoplusia ni, 99
Turnips
  bugs on, 84
  caterpillars on, 107, 117
  flies and maggots on, 157, 162
  millipedes on, 211
  weevils on, 198, 203
Tympanum, for hearing, 5

Varieties, of resistant plants,
  to control insects, 7
Vedalia beetle, 43
Vegetable weevil, 203
Vespula sp., 23
Vision, of insects, 5–6
Vitacea polistiformis, 63

Walkingstick, 152
Walnut caterpillar, 134
Walnut husk fly, 168
Walnuts
  caterpillars on, 100, 109,
    119, 129, 134
  flies and maggots on, 168
  scale on, 188,189
Wasps, 15–16
  as predator. *See* Braconid wasp;
    Chalcid wasp; Ichneumon wasp;
    Mud dauber wasp; Tiphia wasp;
    Trichogramma wasp
  yellow jacket, 23
Water spray, to control insects, 7
Web, as protection for pupa, 3
Webworms. *See* Caterpillars
Weeding, to control insects, 6
Weevils, 195
  apple curculio, 196
  bean, 197
  cabbage curculio, 198
  carrot, 199
  pecan, 200
  plum curculio, 201
  rhubarb curculio, 202
  vegetable, 203
Western tussock moth, 135
Whiteflies, 205–6
  greenhouse, 206
  incomplete metamorphosis of, 3
Whitefringed beetle, 58
Whitelined sphinx moth, 136
Wings, of insects, 1
  development of, 3
  flight and, 6
Wireworms, 207–8
  eastern field, 208
Wood borers. *See* Borers
Woolly apple aphid, 13
Woollybear caterpillar. *See* Yellow
  woollybear caterpillar
Worms. *See* Caterpillars

Yellow jacket, 23
Yellownecked caterpillar, 137
Yellow woollybear caterpillar, 138

Zebra caterpillar, 139
Zonosemata electa, 165

NOTES